Noel Stock
23rd Jan. 1976

EZRA POUND'S PENNSYLVANIA

Compiled for the most part from
Mr. Carl Gatter's researches into
original sources and documents

by

Noel Stock

THE FRIENDS OF THE UNIVERSITY OF
TOLEDO LIBRARIES
1976

FIRST PUBLISHED IN 1976 BY
THE FRIENDS OF THE UNIVERSITY OF TOLEDO LIBRARIES
TOLEDO, OHIO 43606

PREFACE

The title of this book indicates, I think, the principal subject and aim of the contents. The subject is the world in which Ezra Pound grew up; the aim, to give some idea of the part that world played in making him what he was. The book does not pretend to answer any ultimate literary questions. Such questions do not belong to biography: of that I am sure. The book seeks merely to delineate with some accuracy the poet's early environment. It is the product of a collaboration between Carl Gatter and myself lasting (on and off) for more than eight years. There are few words in it that are not based, in some manner, on evidence from the period with which it deals. What Pound or others said, in later years, about this period, was checked against the evidence wherever possible.

The book is not an account of Pound's life: for that I must refer the reader to my Life of Ezra Pound, *wherein the Wyncote years are told in a different way, as prelude to a larger story. The two books sometimes overlap but the differences are considerable. There is much in* Ezra Pound's Pennsylvania *that is completely new, including letters and poetry by Pound, and much detail that might have seemed out of place in the other book.*

A shorter version of Ezra Pound's Pennsylvania *appeared in 1973 in* Poetry Australia *no. 46; I should like to thank the editor, Dr Grace Perry. For permission to use Pound material on that occasion I was indebted to the late Dorothy Pound; for permission on this present occasion I must thank the Trustees of the Ezra Pound Literary Property Trust. I am glad also of this opportunity to record in print my obligation to Leslie W. Sheridan, Director of University of Toledo Libraries, for his decision to publish the book in this form; to the Rare Books Librarian, Lucille B. Emch, who nurtured the idea from the start; and to the Friends of the University of Toledo Libraries, under whose imprint it appears.*

N. S.

Toledo, November 1975

I

Ezra Pound was born in Hailey, Idaho, in 1885, but grew up in Pennsylvania. His father, Homer Loomis Pound, came from Chippewa Falls in Wisconsin; his mother, Isabel Weston, from New York City. While he was still a baby the family moved from Idaho to New York; and on June 11th 1889, his father, who had been in charge of the federal Land Office in Hailey, was appointed an Assistant at the United States Mint in Philadelphia. Thus it was that Pound came to be brought up in Philadelphia and to spend his most formative years, until he was 22, in and around that city. Homer already knew Philadelphia and the mint, having worked there twice before his marriage. His first appointment, as a Temporary Assistant (at $2.51 a day), lasted from April 17th 1881 until June 3rd 1881; and his second appointment, this time as an Assistant, at $3.50 a day, from February 10th 1882 until April 30th 1883. On starting again as an Assistant in 1889 he received $5 a day, until, in April 1891, he was promoted to Assistant Assayer with a salary of $2,000 per annum, with further promotions in 1911 and 1924.

The Pounds lived for about two years in a brick row house with tiny lawn, porch and polished walnut door at 208 South 43rd Street, West Philadelphia, which in those days was at the edge of the city; and then moved ten miles north of Philadelphia to 417 Walnut Street, Jenkintown, on the Reading Railroad. A local newspaper, the *Hatboro Public Spirit*, reported on Saturday, March 22nd 1890: "Mr Pound, of Philadelphia, moved into George W. Tomlinson's new house on Friday." Two doors away was a family by the name of Comley, a member of which was later introduced into canto 28 of Pound's long work *The Cantos*:

Az ole man Comley wd say: Boys! . . .
Never cherr terbakker! Hrwwkke tth!
Never cherr terbakker!

Three doors away on Walnut Street was the Schwarz family, whose daughter, Lula, aged about 12, was, Pound said later, "friendly and protective." Down the hill in West Street were the Schivelys, engaged in the coal and lumber business. Their daughter Nan he "adored" for three years. Later, when she was 16, she spread, he noticed, "to her mother's volume and figure," and eventually married a local young man, Harold Larzelere, elder brother of Pound's school friend and rival, Dayton Larzelere. Leader of the "gang" to which Pound, aged 5, belonged, was a boy named Sheridan. Many years later the poet described him in a letter as "the dashing and heroic and all-competent builder, who put tin roof on hen house etc."

While living in Walnut Street the Pounds attended Grace Presbyterian Church, on the steps of which, he recalled in 1958, he once fell and hurt himself. Next door to the church was a school run by a Miss Elliott which Pound seems to have attended for a year, at least. And his parents were now beginning to take part in local activities. The *Hatboro Public Spirit* of January 17th 1891 records Homer's participation in amateur theatricals: "The Jenkintown Lyceum Association held its annual meeting on Monday night. The following officers were elected for the year: President, H. L. Pound; Vice-Presidents, Rev. Robert Coles and Rev. R. A. Green; Treasurer, A. H. Baker; Secretary, Emma McIntosh." On April 2nd 1892 the paper reported: "Mr Pound moved from Mr Tomlinson's house on Walnut Street to Mr Burrough's house on Hillside Avenue April 1." When Pound was about 7 they moved again to a spacious house not far away at 166 Fernbrook Avenue, Wyncote, close to the Jenkintown railway station. This was Pound's home for the next sixteen years and his parents' for almost forty years. It is not known when exactly they moved to Fernbrook Avenue, but it seems that for some months after the move they rented it on approval. Finally, on July 20th 1893, it was bought, in Isabel Pound's name, from a neighbour, Lewis Leidy, for $6,000. It contained the following rooms. *First or ground floor:* large hall, dining room, front and back parlours, kitchen and pantry. *Second floor:* four bedrooms, two bathrooms, and a sitting room. *Third floor:* three bedrooms, a bathroom, and a storeroom. It was furnished throughout in Victorian style and hung with family portraits, including one of "Uncle Ezry," after whom Pound was named, a William Page portrait of Isabel's mother, Mary Wadsworth Parker, who married Harding Weston, and another of a grandmother or greatgrandmother by the name of How. Later, according to Pound in 1959, some of the furnishings were sold to Henry Ford to help fit up his Wayside Inn.

Restless, even as a child, Pound had no fixed bedroom but at one time or another slept in the "Tower room" and in all three of the bedrooms on the third floor.

Not only was the house comfortable but well-placed in pleasant leafy surroundings which Homer worked to improve and develop. In a letter in 1957 Pound wrote: "Dad planted a row [of trees] down the right side of the yard." These were "pear, peach and cherry." On another occasion he recalled that the cherry and peach produced an edible fruit, and that in the rear garden Homer grew corn and a row of sweet peas "for Isabel." Close to the house at the rear was a large apple tree with a swing.

Wyncote and the surrounding countryside were becoming popular among the rising or newly rich families of Philadelphia. Immediately opposite 166 Fernbrook Avenue a family by the name of Kunkle built a large Victorian house; and two doors away from the Pounds' George Horace Lorimer worked on his *Ladies Home Journal* and sometimes took short cuts through their backyard. Cyrus Curtis, of the *Saturday Evening Post*, also lived nearby and occasionally came to the Pounds' for dinner. In conversation many years later Pound recalled looking over the banister one night when Curtis was there and seeing his "square-cut beard." In November 1898 a local newspaper ran the following note: "The *Saturday Evening Post* is now on sale at the newstand. It is published by C. H. K. Curtis. No comment on its merits is necessary."

Among the families which built their country palaces in or near Wyncote were the Wideners, the Stetsons, the Elkinses and the Wanamakers. But even the arrival of less eminent Philadelphians was recorded with pride in the local press. The *Jenkintown Times* of August 11th 1894 reported: "Mr Kunkle of Philadelphia is going to build a house on Fernbrook Avenue." On November 3rd: "Mr Kunkle's new house is being roofed in." February 16th 1895: "The finishing touches are being put to Mr Kunkle's house on Fernbrook Avenue." March 25th: "Mr Kunkle's house is completed." Two years later, in the issue of March 13th 1897, the paper grew lyrical on the subject:

> Wyncote is just beginning to show its beauty. In the spring of the year, when the grass gets green and the leaves begin to form, with the handsome and elegant buildings amid the trees and shrubbery, this place reminds us of a fairy garden, and parenthetically we might say the fairies are not even lacking. Some of the best known and wealthiest Philadelphia business people live in these elegant mansions, and a person residing here should consider himself blessed as few others are so far as residence location is concerned.

The Pounds, dependent on Homer's salary at the mint, lived simply but well. Isabel, who always kept a maid, was noted in the district for her "high society" voice. Some thought she was impractical but witnesses who knew her well said she was an astute manager. The Pounds were never badly short of money but as the village progressed there were always extra expenses to be met which sometimes placed a strain on them. On one occasion Fernbrook Avenue, which is on a hill, was lowered, and this meant that a retaining wall had to be built. To fit in with this new arrangement Homer had the porch entrance moved from the corner of the house, and also provided a railing.

After the move to Fernbrook Avenue Pound went to the Chelten Hills school in nearby Mather Avenue. The school was run by a well-known Wyncote family called Heacock. One of his best friends as a boy was Edward ("Ned") Heacock who was the same age as Pound and later attended the University of Pennsylvania with him before being drowned on July 24th 1907 in a canoeing accident on a scientific expedition in British Columbia. Pound attended the Heacock's school for a year, until he was about eight. "There are some pleasant memories of it," he wrote in a letter in 1958, "quite a lot in fact." Classes were held originally in the Heacock home, "Netherhouse," on Glenside Avenue, Wyncote; but numbers increased, and in 1892 a school was built on Mather Avenue. From time to time the pupils (according to Annie Heacock's *Reminiscences* of 1926) displayed their talents in "very creditable" performances of "The Bohemian Girl," Tennyson's "The Princess," "Cranford," English songs, Civil War songs, and Negro melodies. What is probably the first published reference to Pound appeared in the school's *Souvenir* of June 1894. It occurs in a long poem which mentions each student in turn:

> Frank Hager, and Dayton, and Lucien
>   Were trying to stand on head,
> But Jay McClure was after them,
>   And so was Heacock's Ned.
>
> Walter Kimber was watching them
>   And not making a single sound,
> Rushton was sucking his finger,
>   And laughing at Ra Pound.

In the family and among his friends Pound was then and for some years known as "Ra" (pronounced *Ray*). From the Heacock establishment he moved to a temporary school run by Miss Florence Ridpath in a house on the southwest corner of Greenwood Avenue (also called Station Road) and Fernbrook Avenue. This was at the bottom of a steep hill, only a short distance from the Pound house. In another letter, written in 1957, he mentioned that "democracy came to Wyncote and it was agreed to desegregate," though he could remember only one Negro family, "the good Miners." He also liked his teacher: "Anyhow, Miss Ridpath made democracy pleasant at the foot of the hill before an official school was erected." Pound remembered a boy by the name of Crosby, who "drew frigates of the revolutionary period in great detail." Attempting to emulate him Pound neglected duty and incurred Miss Ridpath's displeasure; she scolded him. After a long silence Pound announced that he was about to leave, but again Miss Ridpath intervened "in STRONG negative," reserving that decision to her own higher authority. The incident, Pound said, left no scars; he was perfectly conscious of error. Another boy he remembered was Thomas Cochran who went into the Navy. It was possibly this Cochran he had in mind when in 1945 he mentioned racial or hereditary characteristics in canto 79: "Can Grande's grin like Tommy Cochran's." Can Grande was Dante's patron in Verona in the early 14th century. The official school further along Greenwood Avenue, was not so pleasant. One of the teachers ("the indestructible Blanche Summers") "reigned in severity." Also, there was a bad smell from the boys' lavatory in the basement.

In the *Jenkintown Times* these early Wyncote years were recorded, week by week, in leisurely, homely detail. July 7th 1894: "L. C. Leidy and H. L. Pound, employees of the mint, are on their vacation." September 8th 1894: "The public school will be held in Mr Smith's house, corner of Fernbrook and Greenwood Avenues." September 23rd 1894: "Wyncote public school was opened on Monday last with 37 scholars, in charge of Miss Florence Ridpath, of Jenkintown. As the school had only been arranged to accommodate 24 pupils and the books had not arrived the school was dismissed in the morning." September 29th 1894: "At a meeting of the Wyncote Improvement Association Mr Pound spoke in favour of trying to have a sign hung at Jenkintown

Station with Wyncote on it, as Wyncote has been put on the telegraph list." December 8th 1894: "Mrs Pound is in New York on account of the serious sickness of her uncle."

In 1895 the *Times* merged with a competitor, the *Chronicle*, to become the *Jenkintown Times-Chronicle*. On 7th September 1895 it carried a story about the new "official" school: "Wyncote public school opened Monday last with a large attendance of scholars. Mr Kettle of Philadelphia, is principal at present, on account of Miss Passmore being sick." Among the pupils was a boy named Durham. Years later Pound recalled his "great satisfaction" when someone by the name of Gettle[1] shook Durham "like a Javanese puppet." October 26th 1895: "Bicycle riding is becoming quite a rage in Wyncote and vicinity. Many ladies can be seen taking daily rides." December 21st 1895: "J. Howard Hay, the painter, has finished putting the artistic touches upon the house of H. L. Pound." March 21st 1896: "Mrs Cochran has moved into Mr Weber's house on Fernbrook Avenue." May 30th 1896: "Just no more Italians in Wyncote. Is our budding hope that this place will be entirely aristocratic squelched?" February 20th 1897: "Mr and Mrs Pound entertained the Wyncote Musicale on Friday night. An unusually fine programme was given by the members, nearly all of whom were present." May 8th 1897: "H. L. Pound, secretary and treasurer of the Children's Institute, last Wednesday evening, during a prayer meeting in the Presbyterian Church, at Amblers, spoke on the work among the children in the Italian settlement in Philadelphia." September 11th 1897: "Thomas Cochran, Bert Stinson, Ray Pound and Fletcher Hunter will attend the Cheltenham Military Academy this year. The academy opens on the 22nd."

Pound was 11, going on 12, when he entered Cheltenham Military Academy at Ogontz — only a mile or so from his home. There he boarded and wore a cadet uniform. His teacher for Latin and Greek was a Wyncote man, Frederick Doolittle, whom the cadets called "Cassius" or "lean and

---

[1]Possibly he meant the headmaster, Kettle.

11

hungry look." Pound referred to him years later as "a fine bit of old oak."

The one thing about the academy that Pound could not stand was the military drill which formed part of the daily routine. It was described in the academy's catalogue under the heading "Military Drill and Discipline": "The physical training which military drill makes imperative is in itself of great value, securing the best physical culture, a firm and elastic step, erect form, graceful carriage and vigorous bodily powers." The cadets were "schooled in self-restraint and self-mastery, in prompt obedience, in submission to law and authority, and in the exercise of authority under a consciousness of personal responsibility."

Life was not all school, however, and outside with his friends Pound was a normal healthy boy. They played in the surrounding hills, where they had a cave, and climbed and built huts in the Pound apple tree. The cave, by the Tacony Creek, was the subject of a popular poem. The last two lines were remembered, in the 1960s, by an elderly Wyncote resident, Miss Adele M. Polk, who had known Pound as a youth:

> And still on fair Tacony's creek
> Is Juliana's cave.

On one occasion during a flash flood in the creek Pound and another boy were almost drowned while rescuing a dog. Once while practising tennis against the side of the house he broke the stained-glass on the hall landing. The repairs are still visible. Another time, playing baseball, he broke a cellar window belonging to people called Hellerman. He also took up fencing, and he and a boy named Reed were chosen to represent the Military Academy at a fencing display in Philadelphia. During the winter he skated on Wanamaker's Pond at Wyncote (his skill was still remembered many years later) and also went sledding. Fernbrook Avenue with its steep hill immediately outside the Pound house was ideal for this sport.

Pound also enjoyed visiting the Mint, then at the corner of Juniper and Chestnut Streets, Philadelphia, where he was allowed to walk among the machines and talk with the workmen. One day one of the guards pointed to a bag of gold and told him that if he could carry it away he could keep it. It was quite small and looked easy, but when he tried he found it impossible to lift. In his father's office he watched fascinated when a visitor signed a visiting-card and Homer, using a gold-balance, discovered the exact weight of the signature.

The Pounds were closely connected with Calvary Presbyterian Church at Wyncote. Not only did they attend services regularly but Homer taught Sunday School and took part in administrative affairs. Their connection with the Presbyterian Church in the area went back to January 1891 when both Homer and Isabel joined the Grace Presbyterian Church under the Rev. Richard Greene. In declaring his faith Homer explained that he had not been brought up in a religious way and was now joining in the face of family opposition and ridicule. Isabel, already a Presbyterian, presented a certificate to say that she had been a member of the Madison Square church in New York. On moving to Fernbrook Avenue they transferred to the newly-formed Calvary Church; and in *Wyncote Outlines*, a magazine distributed quarterly by Calvary, we find plenty of evidence of their participation in church affairs through the 1890s. Homer was president of the Young People's Society of Christian Endeavour and his wife vice-president of the Women's Union. Homer was one of the speakers in a series of special services and Isabel helped to train Sunday School children in the singing of Christmas carols. In 1894 Homer was elected an elder and, during the next seven or eight years, there were few church activities in which he was not involved.

When they first moved to Fernbrook Avenue the church, a wooden structure, was on the northeast corner of Fernbrook Avenue and Greenwood Avenue, just across from the site of Miss Ridpath's temporary school. In September 1893 the wooden building was rolled to a new site on Bent

13

Road, at the other end of Fernbrook Avenue, with Ezra and his friends accompanying it. The minister of the church was the Rev. Carlos Tracy Chester to whom Pound later dedicated his book of poems, *Exultations,* published in London in 1909. In view of this dedication it is worth noting that Chester published numerous short stories and articles in various newspapers, and between 1889 and 1906 helped edit such publications as *The Booklover's Magazine, Book Monthly,* and the *Sunday School Times.* Some of Pound's interest in writing may have had its beginnings in this man's influence. Chester's son, Hawley, was one of Pound's closest friends. In 1901 the church was taken over by a much more "go ahead" minister, the Rev. William Barnes Lower, whom Ezra did not admire as he did his predecessor. From September 1901 until his marriage in June 1902 Lower lived with the Pounds. Around Philadelphia, and in Presbyterian circles elsewhere, he was well known as a writer of verses; and it is not improbable that he too played some part in directing Pound towards poetry.

Pound's own "profession of faith" in Christianity was made at Calvary on 24th March 1897, when he was 11. He went to church for some years, and once, as a boy, attended a Christian Endeavour convention in Boston. He appears to have drifted away from the practice of his religion during his university days and by the time he was 30, the word "Presbyterian" had become for him a term of abuse. In the poem "L'Homme Moyen Sensuel", written about 1915, he satirized the Rev. Charles Parkhurst, minister at his mother's former church in New York.

Life in Wyncote during the late 1890s seems to have been attended by all the normal joys and irritations of outer-suburbia. Thus we find him at the age of 10 suffering from a sore finger—the result of a game of football; or greatly excited by a visit to Philadelphia to see a minstrel show, which was followed by a further treat—ice-cream at Wanamaker's store. Friendship with the boy Sheip next door was marred somewhat by the latter's bragging: his father, he kept telling Pound, was a man of some substance who man-

Isabel Weston

Left to right: grandfather Thaddeus Coleman Pound , Ezra Pound, his father Homer Pound (standing), and great-grandfather Elijah Pound.

208 South 43rd St., Philadelphia.

417 Walnut St., Jenkintown.

16

166 Fernbrook Ave., Wyncote.

In 1956 Carl Gatter sent Ezra Pound a photograph of the porch and oak at 166 Fernbrook Ave. Pound replied July 18th 1956: "Oak was purty tall in 1900. Wot about the olde apple tree @ the back?"

Wyncote, 1893. Looking south-east from Woodland Ave., with Greenwood Ave. in foreground. 166 Fernbrook Ave. is third from left, back row.

U.S. Mint, Juniper & Chestnut Streets, Philadelphia.

The "new" U.S. Mint, 17th & Spring Garden Streets, Philadelphia.

19

Calvary Presbyterian Church, Wyncote: original wooden building.

SUNDAY-SCHOOL OF THE FIRST ITALIAN PRESBYTERIAN CHURCH, PHILADELPHIA

THE question is often asked, "How shall we reach our Foreign Populations?" A visit to the Tabernacle, at Tenth Street and Washington Avenue, will show **how**, and convince you that it can be done.

A Tent was located here during the Summer of 1903. As a result of the tent work, a Tabernacle was erected, accommodating a thousand persons. A church was organized in October, 1903, which now has a membership of nearly 200, a Sunday-School of 250, a Christian Endeavor Society of 100, and eight young men studying for the Gospel ministry. A Kindergarten and Primary School is conducted five days each week. Almost daily children apply for admission into the School, but are turned away for lack of room. Already parents have applied to have their children entered next fall.

Parents appreciate the interest of the teachers in their children. Homes are thus opened to "house-to-house" visitors and Bible readers. Entire families now attend the church services, becoming interested through the children at school. "A little child shall lead them."

The First Italian Presbyterian Church, 10th St. &
Washington Ave., Philadelphia.

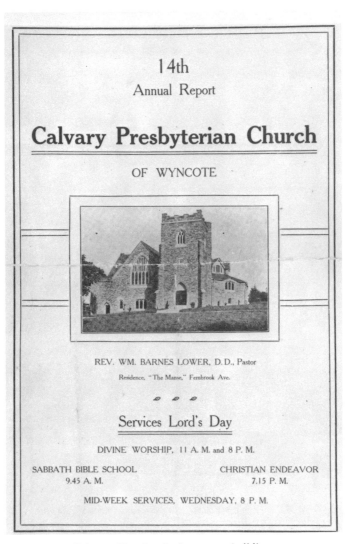

14th
Annual Report

Calvary Presbyterian Church

OF WYNCOTE

REV. WM. BARNES LOWER, D. D., Pastor

Residence, "The Manse," Fernbrook Ave.

Services Lord's Day

DIVINE WORSHIP, 11 A. M. and 8 P. M.

SABBATH BIBLE SCHOOL
9.45 A. M.

CHRISTIAN ENDEAVOR
7.15 P. M.

MID-WEEK SERVICES, WEDNESDAY, 8 P. M.

Calvary Church: the later stone building.

Miss Elliott's school, Old York Rd., Jenkintown. Pound looked for it in vain when he drove north along York Rd. in 1958. The building had been demolished in 1938.

Chelten Hills School, Mather Ave., Wyncote.

Miss Ridpath's "temporary" school, Fernbrook and Greenwood Avenues.

Miss Florence Ridpath. From an album belonging to the Old York Rd. Historical Society, Abington Library, Jenkintown.

23

Ezra Pound, aged 9.

On the porch at Miss Ridpath's "temporary" school, early in spring, 1895, when Pound was 9. *Back row* (left to right): Harold Washburn, of Maple Ave., whose father was local postmaster; Horace Faust; Miss Ridpath; identity of next two unknown; a boy by the name of Luskin, whose family ran a grocery store at north-west corner of Glenside & Greenwood Avenues; Jimmy Luskin; Ezra Pound; Tom Cochran, who lived next door to Pound.

Middle row: Dayton Larzelere, who lived on Washington Lane — his father was a wealthy lawyer; Lotti Shoemaker; Mary Washburn, who became postmistress of Wyncote when her father left town never to return; Mary Shoemaker; Maggie Luskin.

Front row: Anna Corts, whose father was a machinist & inventor; Mary Permar; Anna Baird, whose father was known locally as "a good carpenter"; Emma Hellerman, whose father, Frank, worked at the switchworks.

Wyncote Elementary or "official" school.

Cheltenham Military Academy Catalogue; cadets on manoeuvre.

Pound at Cheltenham Military Academy, 1898.

ufactured cigar-boxes. One of the things Pound liked was to ride in a buggy hired from Levi Bean who ran the local livery stable in Greenwood Avenue almost immediately opposite the bottom of Fernbrook Avenue. Bean was one of the original members of Calvary Church and a great favourite with the young boys because he would sometimes allow them to help with the harnessing of his horses. Another attraction at the stable was a contraption which enabled Bean to lift a carriage or cart from the Greenwood Avenue level to a loft above: it could then be driven out onto a road running along the hill behind the stable. Edward Hicks Parry, of Wyncote, in a letter dated December 8th 1973, wrote the following account of his brother Ellwood and Levi Bean:

> Ellwood hired a horse and single sleigh one Sunday afternoon in the cold and snowy January of 1893, and took father and seven-year-old brother Carle out for an hour-and-a-half. "It was a very pleasant ride," he confided to his diary. On two other occasions, "unable to resist the allurements of a sleigh ride," he favoured his sister and two brothers. An hour "cost but a dollar, which I thought very reasonable." On yet another afternoon he paid but fifty cents, "the rig was not quite as stylish as some."
>
> During the same record-making month of winter weather, Ellwood and sister Anna were taken by Mr Bean or his helper to an evening dancing class at Heacock's. Snow was melting on the 26th, "but by keeping well to the side of the road, the sleigh slipped along very nicely." A week later, the conveyance was a wagon. Whether wagon or sleigh, the charge was alway ten cents per person per ride

Nor was life devoid of artistic interludes. The *Times-Chronicle* of October 30th 1897, reported that "On Friday evening, October 29th, at 8 p.m., the ladies of Calvary Presbyterian Church were instrumental in having presented

some old English ballads, illustrated by tableaux at Heacock's Hall." And there was even a rumour, published in
1898, that an opera house was shortly to be built in the
village. On 19th March 1898 the paper proudly announced
that a member of the Pound family had ventured into
authorship: "An article from the pen of H. L. Pound of this
place appears on the fourth page of this issue." The article
was elaborately headed, as follows:

WHERE TO FIND GOLD

Homer L. Pound Points Out
Places in This Country Better
Than Klondyke

Easier to Prospect

No Such Risks Need Be Encountered
Which Are Met in the Alaskan
Territory—The Great Gold Production
of the United States

As the year 1897-8 came to a close at the Military
Academy Pound took part in the annual athletic meeting.
In the high jump he was beaten by Dayton Larzelere. But
at the festivities afterwards he managed to eat innumerable
cakes and sweets and drink large quantities of lemonade.

During the school holidays Pound often visited his rela-
tives in New York including his grandmother Mary Weston.
In the summer of 1898 an aunt by marriage, Frances
Weston, whom he called Aunt Frank, took him and his
mother to England and Europe for his first inspection of
London, Paris and Italy. Their departure and the fact that
Homer went to stay at the nearby town of Meadowbrook
were both recorded in the *Times-Chronicle*. Although the
trip was to have lasting effects on Pound's life and poetry,
things went on as usual in Wyncote after their return in
September, with Homer busy about his Christian Endeavour
work, Homer and Isabel attending a lecture by a visiting

professor on "Modern Literature", Homer speaking at a Republican meeting at Ogontz, Homer and Isabel entertaining the Wyncote "Round About Club" at their home, Homer, in 1900, attending the Republican National Convention with his father, Thaddeus, who was an alternate delegate from Wisconsin, and Homer being elected director of the Wyncote public school. Occasionally there were special treats. The *Times-Chronicle* carried the following story on 25th November, 1899: "Fletcher Hunter and Ra Pound report having a good time last Saturday evening. The Cheltenham Military Academy gave all the boys an 'oyster ride'. They drove over to Indian Rock Hotel and had an oyster supper. It took two large buses to take them over and back." The same issue reported that "Mrs Pound sent the Cheltenham football team a large chocolate cake, which was very much appreciated by the team".

Pound's studies at the academy included Latin, Greek, English and Arithmetic. He did not graduate (he seems to have left under a cloud) but moved on to a high school, possibly the Cheltenham Township High School at Elkins Park only a short distance from Wyncote. He was not, however, listed as a member of the school's graduating class in the *Times-Chronicle's* report (June 22nd 1901) of the commencement exercises. A few years later Homer Pound sat as one of the school's directors and was among those responsible for the construction of a completely new school in 1905.

II

After spending part of the summer of 1901 at Ocean City with his parents Pound entered the University of Pennsylvania in the autumn of that year, shortly before his sixteenth birthday. Among the subjects he studied in his first year were English Composition, Public Speaking, Algebra, German Grammar, American Colonial History, Principles of Government in the United States, and Latin. For English his teachers were Dr. Felix E. Schelling, Dr. Clarence G. Child, and Dr. Cornelius Weygandt. He corresponded with Schelling and Weygandt occasionally in later years and referred to them once or twice in his work. His Latin teacher, Walton Brooks McDaniel, recalled many years later that Pound sat at the back of the class "to be independent of excessive *ex-cathedra* observation". His History teacher was Dr. Herman Vandenburg Ames whose ability he paid tribute to, thirty years later, when from Rapallo, Italy, he sent a contribution to the Herman Vandenburg Ames memorial volume published by the University of Pennsylvania Press in 1936. In a Foreword the editors of the book explained that "On May 7, 1935, a memorial meeting was held . . . at the University of Pennsylvania where many gathered to pay final tribute." Pound's contribution was identified as from "Ezra Pound, College '05, Rapallo, Italy, April 8, 1935" and included the following: "I don't remember how long he had been teaching in 1901, 1902, and there may be students with longer memories, but this note and the one that missed him, at least prove over and above any mere opinion that his courses had a vitality outlasting the mere time of lectures. After thirty years I still have pleasant recollections of 'Reconstruction' and 'Foreign Relations' courses. . . . The idea that a student might have a legitimate curiosity was in no way alien to his (Dr Ames') sensibilities." One of Pound's companions in Ames's class was a tall Philadelphian, James Dougherty Kirkbride. One day as the result of student horseplay Kirkbride was sent sprawling in front of Ames as the latter entered the classroom. Ames waited, without comment, until the way had been cleared, and then swept forward. This was, according to Pound, a good example of his sense of proportion.

With his mother and father Pound spent the New Year holiday of 1901-2 visiting members of the family in New York; and at the end of his first university year he went with his parents on a second visit to Europe. They were away from about June 16th until September 20th, and visited England, France and Italy. On October 4th the *Times-Chronicle* reported: "Homer L. Pound, chief assayer in the United States Mint in Philadelphia, with his family, arrived in New York from Europe on the steamship St. Paul on Saturday, September 20. They had a splendid trip across the Atlantic on the home voyage. The gentleman and his family returned to their home in Wyncote last Saturday greatly pleased with their summer abroad." The paper also recorded the fact that W. B. Hackenburg, president of the Jewish Hospital Association, who had been occupying the Pound house during the summer, returned to Philadelphia in September.

When Pound began his second university year in the autumn of 1902 he went to live in a dormitory. His courses included Nineteenth Century English Novelists, Ethics, Latin, and two of the courses remembered in his memorial note on Ames: "Foreign Relations of the United States" and "The Civil War and Reconstruction". Among the friends and acquaintances he made at this time were the following students: Lewis Burtron Hessler of 4009 Chestnut

31

Street, Philadelphia, with whom he corresponded in later years; Henry Slonimsky, a student of philosophy, whom he met again in London and Paris c. 1913; Joseph Bromley, whose skill with tobacco-juice was mentioned by Pound years later in canto 28; and Alfred de Forest Snively, 63rd and Market Streets, Philadelphia, whose parents he met a few years later in Venice.

But his best friend was an artist William Brooke Smith whose knowledge of painting, ceramics and other arts was mental nourishment the like of which Pound had never before encountered. Between 1896 and 1899, a William B. Smith lived at 1612 Diamond Street, North Philadelphia. This was a large, fashionable brownstone row house, two blocks west of Broad Street, and just north of Temple University. But the first definite news we have of Pound's friend is in 1902 when he became a student at the Philadelphia College of Art ("School of Industrial Art") at the corner of Broad and Pine Streets in central Philadelphia. That year he received a Class A certificate for industrial drawing and in 1904 a Class B certificate in Applied Design. He received his diploma from the college in 1905. From 1904 until 1908 he lived at 839 North Franklin Street, a large semi-detached town-house in Philadelphia. It is possible he also lived for a time at 1624 Park Avenue, a small row house directly behind a group of large Victorian houses on Broad Street. From both of these addresses he wrote Pound letters dealing with literature and art. When he died in 1908 Pound paid tribute by dedicating to him his first book, *A Lume Spento*, published by the author at his own expense in Venice in June of that year. The dedication, spaced out over a full page, in a variety of type-faces, reads: "This book was La Fraisne (The Ash Tree) dedicated to such as love this same beauty that I love, somewhat after mine own fashion. But sith one of them has gone out very quickly from amongst us it is given A Lume Spento (With Tapers Quenched) in memoriam eius mihi caritate primus William Brooke Smith Painter, Dreamer of Dreams." In a letter from Paris in 1921 Pound said that Smith had been remarkable for his knowledge. "I haven't replaced him", he wrote, "and shan't and no longer hope to." According to Frank Ankenbrand, Jr., who in 1928-9 boarded with Homer and Isabel Pound, there was a small (6" x 4") water-colour by Smith in the front bedroom on the third floor of 166 Fernbrook Avenue. Ezra's two foils and fencing mask were in a corner of the same room. This period of Pound's life, in which Smith played such an important part, was largely given over to what may perhaps be called aestheticism: with just those touches of affectation and preciosity we might expect of a young man of talent, who, in his struggle to see beyond his parents' world, has gravitated towards "artistic" companions. It was to these years that he owed the threads and echoes from Pater's *Appreciations* and Wilde's *Intentions* which appear later in his work.

One reason why he spent so much time in Philadelphia is that during these years his parents spent a good deal of time there too, working among the children and the poor in the Italian section. When they did not settle in the Wyncote house after their 1902 trip abroad, there were rumours that they had left for good, especially after the Sessional Body of Calvary church, meeting on January 7th 1903, regretfully accepted the resignation of "Our brother and fellow Presbyter, Homer L. Pound," who, "feeling impelled by a divine call," is entering upon "institutional work in the city of Philadelphia". The resolutions of the evening, carried unanimously, praised in the highest terms his "many years of faithful service". Ten days later the *Times-Chronicle* printed this story: "The matter of Homer L. Pound's residence has been cleared up, he having declared this week that he is still a resident of Wyncote and that he and his family expect to again occupy their home here after May 5th, which time the lease of his house expires." In actual fact they returned during the first week of April 1903, earlier than expected; but moved back again to Philadelphia later that year, leaving the house, for the second summer running, in the hands of Mr Hackenburg of the Jewish Hospital Association. On May 9th 1903 the *Times-Chronicle* reported that "Captain Emily Hester, of Slum Post No. 1, Philadelphia, spent two days this week with her friend Mrs

H. L. Pound. The captain . . . has seen many years of service in the Army, and is a personal friend of General Booth and his family."

By the time he began his second year at the university Pound was composing verse. Although much of what he then wrote has disappeared we know from Pound himself that his first published work was a poem on a "political" theme which appeared in the *Jenkintown Times-Chronicle*. He could not remember what exactly it was about or when exactly it appeared. But a search of the files of the *Times-Chronicle* has brought to light an unsigned piece which is probably the one in question. Called "Ezra on the Strike" it is based upon the coal strike of 1902, which, as it progressed from November into December, left Philadelphia seriously short of coal for heating, so that some families closed their houses and went to apartment buildings or hotels. The Philadelphia newspapers reported "much distress among the poor." The poem appeared in the *Times-Chronicle* of November 8th; the lines are spoken by an old farmer on his way to town:

> Wal, Thanksgivin' do be comin' round.
> With the price of turkeys on the bound,
> And coal, by gum! Thet were just found,
>   Is surely gettin' cheaper.
> The winds will soon begin to howl,
> And winter, in its yearly growl,
> Across the medders begin to prowl,
>   And Jack Frost gettin' deeper.
>
> By shucks! It seems to me,
> That you and I orter be
> Thankful, that our Ted could see
>   A way to operate it.
> I sez to Mandy, sure, sez I,
> I'll bet that air patch o' rye,
> Thet he'll squash 'em by-and-by,
>   And he did, by cricket!
>
> No use talkin', he's the man —
> One of the best that ever ran,

Fer didn't I turn Republican
    One o' the fust?
I 'lowed as how he'd beat the rest,
But old Si Perkins, he hemmed and guessed,
And sed as how it wuzn't best
    To meddle with the trust.

Now Pattison, he's gone up the flue,
And Coler, he kinder got there, tew,
So Si, put thet in your cud to chew,
    And give us all a rest.
Now thet I've had my little say
I wish you all a big Thanksgivin' day,
While I plod on to town with hay,
    And enjoy it best.

Although most of the evidence suggests that this is Pound's composition, one small doubt remains. William Barnes Lower published a number of similar poems, both signed and unsigned, in the *Times-Chronicle,* about the same time, and it is just possible that "Ezra on the Strike" was from his pen. However, when some of his poems, including those that appeared in the *Times-Chronicle* in November 1902, were collected in 1954 under the title *Falling Petals,* "Ezra on the Strike" was not among them.

It was while he was at university during the year 1902-3 that Pound formed one of his most lasting literary friendships — that with the poet William Carlos Williams. Williams was several years older than Pound; at first he studied Dentistry and later Medicine. Brought together by another student because they both wrote verse, he and Pound remained friends, despite strong disagreements, until Williams's death more than half a century later. During the early days of their friendship Williams was amazed at Pound's knowledge of literature and had great admiration for his determination to devote his life to it. In an article in the *New York Evening Post Literary Review* of February 19th 1927 Williams wrote: "Ezra Pound found it hard going at Penn. He seemed then to be one of the few who have made out what life is about . . . And so at Penn, while Schelling dogmatically expounded upon the theory of blank verse in the plays of William Shakespeare, Pound would be turning the pages of his own priceless manuscripts or, forbidden that adjustment he would take out an immense tin watch and wind it with elaborate deliberation. This was Pound at his best in the puppy stage."[1]

One of the biggest events of the university year 1902-3 was the playing of Euripides's *Iphigenia among the Taurians* by undergraduates. As early as May 27th 1902 the student daily newspaper *The Pennsylvanian* published a story that "Plans are actively progressing for the production of a Greek play next year." In an editorial on October 16th the paper said: "It is with pleasure that we see active preparations being made in the direction of holding the Greek play in the near future. As we have no doubt said before, this production will have a great influence upon the general university world of the East, and will give Pennsylvania further prestige in literary and classic circles." By February 1903 rehearsals were under way and on March 12th the paper announced that "A very important meeting of the chorus members of the Greek play will be held tomorrow evening at 1123 Chestnut Street." During the final week before the two performances the cast and chorus rehearsed every evening; and when the day of the first performance, April 28th, arrived, *The Pennsylvanian* carried a front-page photograph of the cast and chorus and an outline of the play. Listed among the fifteen chorus members was E. W. L. Pound (the W. L. standing for Weston Loomis, names of other branches of the family). So great was the excitement that Mrs. Frances A. Weston ("Aunt Frank") and a friend of the family, Dr. Jas. L. Beyer (possibly the "Ole Byers" mentioned in canto 28), came all the way from New York to see Ezra perform. The programme described the event as follows:

---

[1] I owe this quotation to Eric Homberger's collection, *Ezra Pound,* in the Critical Heritage series (London & Boston 1972).

TRANSLATION

OF THE

IPHIGENIA AMONG THE TAURIANS

OF EURIPIDES

AS PERFORMED AT THE ACADEMY OF MUSIC
IN PHILADELPHIA

April 28th and 29th, 1903

BY UNDERGRADUATES OF THE
UNIVERSITY OF PENNSYLVANIA

UNDER THE DIRECTION OF

THE DEPARTMENT OF GREEK

WITH MUSIC COMPOSED BY

PROFESSOR HUGH ARCHIBALD CLARKE

OF THE UNIVERSITY

In the audience was William Carlos Williams who many years later said that Pound, in a large blonde wig, threw his arms about and heaved his breast "in ecstasies of extreme emotion." Next day *The Pennsylvanian* reported a large crowd and said the play had been "Very Well Received." Of the chorus it remarked: "Through all of the play, except a few lines at the beginning, the chorus members are on stage. The gestures were not at all times animated, but both these and the dances were gone through with care and some grace, which met with the due appreciation of the audience."

Pound's other university activities included chess, fencing and football. In March 1903 he was a member of the nine-man Pennsylvania chess team which drew 5-5 with Princeton; Pound lost to his Princeton opponent. He took fencing lessons from the university coach but is not listed as a member of the 1903 team. As for football, he did not play but liked to watch, and is said to have acted as a voluntary usher at Franklin field. The extent to which university sporting activities impressed themselves on his mind may be gauged from an article, "How I Began," which he published in *T.P.'s Weekly*, London, in June 1913. There he described

THE FRESHMAN CLASS

The Freshman Class, University of Pennsylvania, 1902. Pound is first from left, back row, wearing a cap.

Pound, aged 16.

Class Day, University of Pennsylvania, 1902.

College Hall, University of Pennsylvania, as it was when Pound attended.

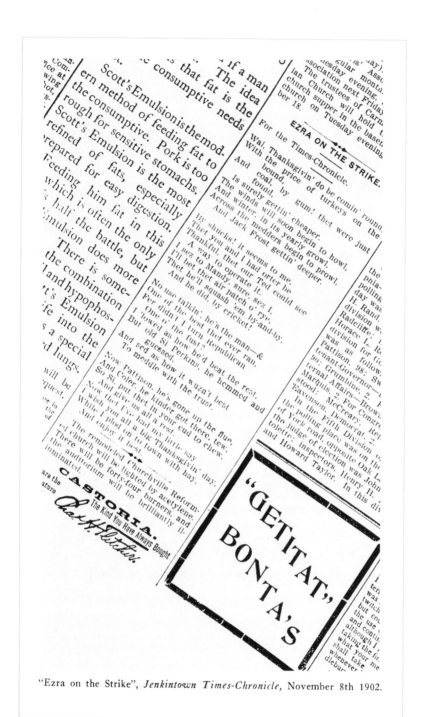

"Ezra on the Strike", *Jenkintown Times-Chronicle*, November 8th 1902.

The Pennsylvanian

L. XIX.—No. 152   PHILADELPHIA, TUESDAY, APRIL 28, 1903.   PRICE, TWO CE

Athena also directs that the eb
be sent back to Greece, since th
her wish. Theus consents, for
can oppose the will of the go
And so, with the exit song of
chorus, the play comes to an en
The characters will be playe
follows:

THE CAST.

King .... Milton B. Stell
Orestes .... William O. M
Pylades .... Robert T. M
Herdsman ...... Thomas E. Ro
Messenger .... Robert B
Iphigenia ...... Frank V. H. S
Athena ..... George W. McClell

CHORUS.

C. W. Gaul, leader; C. C.
vester, P. R. Stockman, F.
Pritchett, L. B. Deck, A. A. Gr
ocke, E. W. L. Pound, R. S. Dick
G. C. Foust, E. F. Hitchcock, W
Nelson, M. A. Nields, F. C. Stil
M. R. Van Cleve, W. S. Watson.
Piper.—F. M. Gray.
Attendant to Iphigenia.—J.
Huggins.
Temple Attendants.—G. V. E
kins, H. H. Harter, G. H. Wa
Jr., C. L. Downing.
Barbarian Guards.—F. L. Cl
W. C. Pugh, W. L. Hemphill, M.
Jacobs, E. S. McCartney, J. Lisle
M. Thissell.
Herdsmen.—E. W. Chadwick,
E. Lamberton, J. A. Snyder.

Courtesy of "The Evening Bulletin.

CAST AND CHORUS OF THE GREEK PLAY.

THE GREEK PLAY.

sented at the Academy of Mus c
This Evening.

'Iphigenia Among the Taurians,'
ich has been in preparation for
h a great while, will be presented
the first time in America this

skulls, forms the back scene. While
Iphigenia is preparing a sacrifice in
the temple Orestes and Pylades appear. Orestes, commanded by the
oracle, had slain his mother, because
she had murdered his father, Aga-
memnon, on his return from Troy.
But he is tormented by the Furies,

know that she is still alive. So she
promises to let Orestes go in safety
if he will take the letter, but he re-
fuses to save himself at the expense
of Pylades. Finally it is agreed that
Pylades is to go and Orestes to remain and die. Iphigenia comes out
of the temple with the letter and

The student newspaper on the day of the Greek play. Pound is in the back row, second from left.

Ezra Pound (second from left) as captive Greek maiden in Euripides's *Iphigenia among the Taurians,* 1903.

41

TRANSLATION

OF THE

IPHIGENIA AMONG THE TAURIANS

OF EURIPIDES

AS PERFORMED AT THE ACADEMY OF MUSIC
IN PHILADELPHIA

APRIL 28TH AND 29TH, 1903

BY UNDERGRADUATES OF THE UNIVERSITY OF PENNSYLVANIA

UNDER THE DIRECTION OF

THE DEPARTMENT OF GREEK

WITH MUSIC COMPOSED BY

PROFESSOR HUGH ARCHIBALD CLARKE

OF THE UNIVERSITY

Pound

42

William Carlos Williams,
The Scope, 1906.

Williams as member of the University of Pennsylvania fencing team.

Williams (with long white beard) as Polonius in University of Pennsylvania production of *Mr Hamlet of Denmark*, 1905.

Lewis Burtron Hessler.

Pound at Hamilton, 1905.

Hamilton College, Clinton, N.Y.

46

Belangal Alba

EX. MANUSCRIPT OF TENTH CENTURY, TRANSLATED.

PHOEBUS shineth e'er his glory flyeth,
Aurora drives faint light athwart the land,
And the drowsy watcher cryeth,
"Arise!"

REF:—
Dawn light, o'er sea and height, riseth bright,
Passeth vigil, clear shineth on the night.

They be careless of the gates, delaying,
Whom the ambush glides to hinder
Whom I warn and cry to, praying,
"Arise!"

REF:—
O'er cliff and ocean white dawn appeareth,
Passeth vigil, and the shadows cleareth.

Forth from out Arcturus, North Wind bloweth
Stars of heaven sheathe their glory
And, Sun-driven, forth-goeth
Settentrion.

REF:—
O'er sea-mist and mountain is dawn display'd,
It passeth watch and maketh night afraid.

—*E. P.*

The Hamilton Literary Magazine, May 1905.

Ezra Weston Pound, Philadelphia, Pa.
"Ezra"
"Bib's" pride. Leader of the anvil chorus at
the Commons. Oh, how he throws those
legs! Peroxide blonde.

The Hamiltonian, 1905.

POUND   RICHARDSON   DRISCOLL   TOLL

Pound as member of the chess team, *The Hamiltonian,* 1906.

48

how thrilled he had been in coming to London, able to meet men who were not only poets themselves but had known important writers of the past, or were able to pass on stories told about great men by friends or contemporaries: "Besides knowing living artists I have come in touch with the tradition of the dead. I have had in this the same sort of pleasure that a schoolboy has in hearing of the star plays of former athletes. I have renewed my boyhood. I have repeated the sort of thrill that I used to have in hearing of the deeds of T. Truxton Hare; the sort that future freshmen will have in hearing how 'Mike' Bennett stopped Weeks."

T. Truxton Hare, who was a student at the University of Pennsylvania while Pound was there, was a brilliant athlete — captain of the football team 1899-1900 and a member of the Olympic track team in 1900. He died in 1956. Michael Smith Bennett, known as "Mike," was also a student at the university during Pound's time there; he played football, baseball and basketball. He died in 1964. As for the third sportsman, Weeks, there are two possibilities: there was a Henry Conner Weeks, who played water polo, cricket[1] and other sports, and a Stephen Merrill Weeks, who was an oarsman but does not seem to have rowed for Pennsylvania.

During these years when Pound was at university, stories were heard at Wyncote about his having been ducked in a pond by other students. One such story, recounted half a century later by a classmate, F. Granville Munson, was that Pound unwittingly joined in a ritual march by senior students, which was forbidden to lower classmen, and was thrown into a muddy lily pond in the botanical garden for his trouble. Another version was published in the magazine *Arts in Philadelphia* in May 1940: "Ezra's habiliments offended his classmates, who showed their disfavour by removing the [bright coloured] socks and throwing them and Ezra into the 'frog pond' in the botany gardens. It is

[1]In those days a Philadelphia cricket team played against England; and at least one American became an outstanding bowler and batsman in English county cricket.

recorded that he cursed his classmates in seven languages and returned the next day wearing the offending socks." This same article, headed "Ezra Pound of Wyncote," claims that he was one day heard to say to "one of the most important professors at the university, 'Shaw is greater than Shakespeare'." The affair of the socks was recorded in the *Jenkintown Times-Chronicle* not long after it occurred, but no name was mentioned. It appeared on April 19th 1902 in the section headed "Wyncote Whispers": "The U. of P. students haven't any use for loudness in half-hose. They compelled one of their number to adopt Nature's own 'flesh colour' en route to our village. The thermometer registered about forty degrees. He is doing well."

Pound's scholastic record during his freshman and sophomore years was quite undistinguished; only in one of his mathematics courses did he appear to his teacher to be above average. Some of the things he learnt in his mathematics classes seem to have hung in his mind. In an article "The Wisdom of Poetry" published in the New York magazine *Forum* in April 1912 he wrote: "A certain man named Plarr and another man whose name I have forgotten, some years since, developed the functions of a certain obscure sort of equation, for no cause save their own pleasure in the work. The applied science of their day had no use for their deductions, a few sheets of paper covered with arbitrary symbols — without which we should have no wireless telegraph. What the analytical geometer does for space and form, the poet does for the states of consciousness." He continued throughout his career to use ideas and analogies from mathematics.

It was partly as a result of his poor progress at the University of Pennsylvania that in 1903 he transferred to Carlos Tracy Chester's old college, Hamilton, at Clinton, in upper New York State. (Another reason for the move was that his parents were not happy about the company he was keeping in Philadelphia.) At Hamilton he spent two years studying Latin, French, Italian, Provençal, Anglo-Saxon, etc., and in June 1905 received his Ph.B.

Pound was away at Hamilton when W. B. Yeats, by then a renowned figure in English literature, lectured at the University of Pennsylvania on November 23rd 1903. Pound did not meet Yeats until 1909, in London; but it is possible he derived some of his early interest in him from one of his University of Pennsylvania teachers, Cornelius Weygandt. Pound studied under Weygandt as a freshman and sophomore and also when he returned for graduate work. According to *The Pennsylvanian* of November 21st 1903, "A certain special interest attaches to the visit of Mr Yeats, owing to the fact that he entertained Dr Cornelius Weygandt, of the English Department, as his guest during Dr Weygandt's stay in Ireland a year ago, and gave him every assistance in collecting material for his study of contemporary English poetry." Another poet whom Pound certainly owed to Weygandt's teaching was Yeats's friend Lionel Johnson. A lecture on Johnson, dated 1905, may be found in Weygandt's book *Tuesdays at Ten: A Garnering from the Talks of Thirty Years on Poets, Dramatists and Essayists*, published in Philadelphia in 1928.

In May 1904 Homer Pound went to Buffalo, as a Commissioner from the Presbytery of Philadelphia, to attend the 116th annual General Assembly of the Presbyterian Church. On his way home he stopped off at Hamilton to see his son. Relations between them were sometimes strained at this stage because Homer's cheques barely covered Pound's expenses and were sometimes slow to arrive. In a letter written to his father from Hamilton, Pound explained that he had paid for books, carpet, coal and stove out of $20 already received; but he needed another $90, he said, for items which he listed as follows:

Commons	between $50 and $52
Room	$ 6
Contingent	$ 8
Tuition	$25
Books	$ 8
	$97

For part of the time that Pound was at Hamilton his parents lived at 502 South Front Street, Philadelphia. During the winter of 1903-4 they worked among the poor at the College Settlement House in Philadelphia. Homer was also super-intendent of the First Italian Presbyterian church in Phila-delphia and Isabel his organist. On one occasion Homer divided a large shell collection among the urchins. By mid-September 1904 they were back at 166 Fernbrook Avenue where Isabel took two boarders, a Miss Whitechurch and a Mrs Mary Lovell, whom she referred to as her "paying guests."

Among Pound's published poems there is at least one which appears to have been written in 1905 as the result of a friendship at the University of Pennsylvania. It is called "For E.McC" and was composed following the early death of a fellow-student, Eugene McCartney, who was Pound's "counter-blade" under the university fencing coach, Signor Leonardo Terrone. McCartney, according to Pound's poem, was "Struck of the blade that no man parrieth," but lived on in the memories of his friends:

So art thou with us, being good to keep
In our heart's sword-rack, though thy sword-arm sleep.

In September 1905 Pound took part in several tennis tournaments in Wyncote. The following memories are from a letter by Edward Hicks Parry to Mr Carl Gatter, dated November 2nd 1973. The part dealing with tennis is based upon a record, "Lawn Tennis on the Parry Court, Wyncote," which Mr Parry wrote down in 1905:

One fleeting view of Pound remains in my memory uneffaced or blurred after many, many years. On a Sunday afternoon, my brother Carle and I chanced to see him cresting over the top of our Woodland Road hill and sloping down to the Proctor house, which at that time was next door. He looked quite dudefied, we thought, with his gloves and hat and cane. Doubtless, we agreed, he came a-courting . . . Before that Sunday I had had a nodding acquaintance with Ray — as we called him in our Wyncote youth — and even, perhaps, had experienced my closest association with him. It was tennis that brought us together — and for hours at a time. Since he was quite a tennis enthusiast all his life, surely something should be added here concerning his Wyncote matches.

Mr Chester — the Rev. Carlos Chester, but we lads addressed him as Mister — had a court next to his dwelling on what is now Heacock Lane. His son, Hawley, was a pal of mine, so it was natural that I should steal away at times from our grass court at 119 Woodland to try my luck on his clay one.

On September 19th 1905 Ray beat Mr Chester, 6-1, 6-0, and I, Hawley, 6-4, 6-4. Thus Ray and I met in the semi-finals, he outlasting me, 3-6, 6-1, 10-8. In the finals, on the 20th, Ray lost to Ned Rogers in straight sets. In the doubles, on the 25th, Ray and Donald Dietrich defeated Hawley and me, 2-6, 8-6, 6-4. Ray and Donald were outclassed in the finals, losing to Frank and Karl Rogers, 6-2, 6-3, 6-2.

Ray's parents were very fond and proud of their one chick. Homer Pound I was acquainted with from my public school days, he coming at times to address us, and subsequently, when I was commuting to jobs in Philadelphia, our ways would occasionally merge. He was remarkably approachable, interesting and friendly. I may have seen Mrs Pound somewhat oftener. She was a member in its early years of the Wyncote Bird Club, which, of course, I haunted. She, too, was unfailingly cordial. But, of imposing presence, and rustling in her silks and satins, she was a Grand Lady, and I but a poor, shy, country lad!

When Pound returned to the University of Pennsylvania in the autumn of 1905, to study for his master's degree, he concentrated on Spanish literature, Old French, Provençal, Italian and Latin. His teachers included Dr Hugo A. Rennert, Professor of Romance Languages and Literature, and Walton Brooks McDaniel, Assistant Professor of Latin. Rennert was later mentioned by Pound in canto 28 and also in his prose work *The Spirit of Romance* (1910). As author of a scholarly *Life of Lope de Vega* Rennert influenced considerably Pound's view of the great Spanish poet, as can be seen from the chapter devoted to Lope in *The Spirit of Romance*.[1] There is a tradition at the University of Pennsylvania, associated with the name of Clarence Child, that the poet's well-known parody, "Ancient Music":

> Winter is icummen in,
> Lhude sing Goddam . . .

was originally uttered, or began to take shape, during his graduate years.

Among Pound's friends at this time was Hilda Doolittle, daughter of Charles Doolittle, the university's Professor of Astronomy and director of the Flower Astronomical Observatory at Upper Darby which was then in the country. In the article "Ezra Pound of Wyncote," from which I have already quoted, is is said that Pound met Hilda at a fancy-dress Hallowe'en party:

> He wore a green robe, a souvenir of his visit to Tunis. The robe was the subject of much discussion as it set off Ezra's "Gozzoli bronze-gold hair." "I had a friend," writes Hilda Doolittle, "whose favourite sister was suffering from stupid nerve-specialists. Ezra was terribly upset about it and wanted something to be done. The girl herself was desperate and Ezra one day said: 'Don't you think Matilda might like that green coat?' He insisted on her accepting the priceless robe — just to cheer her up."

With a group of friends Pound and Miss Doolittle often went for woodland walks near the observatory and some-

---

[1] For an account of Pound's graduate courses, based on University of Pennsylvania records, see Emily Mitchell Wallace's "Penn's Poet Friends" in *The Pennsylvania Gazette* (February 1973).

times held parties and musical evenings at 166 Fernbrook Avenue. For a time he and Hilda were unofficially engaged, and the young poet composed a number of songs in her honour. He later typed these and other poems—twenty-five all told — then bound them in vellum and presented them to Hilda under the title *Hilda's Book.* A few of the poems, and passages from a handful of others, appeared later among his published verse. But most of them remain unpublished. They are mostly rather laboured, as the young poet himself apparently saw, but occasionally the movement is interesting:

> Wherefore take thou my laboured
> > litany
> Halting, slow pulsed it is,
> > being the lees
> Of song wine that the master
> > bards of old
> Have left for me to drink
> > thy glory in.

Another of the unpublished ones called "Ver Novum," contains this attempt to catch the music of the sea:

> Marescent, fading on the
> > dolorous brink
> That maketh cliff border to
> > that marasmic sea
> Where all desire's harmony
> Tendeth and endeth in
> > sea monotone . . .

Although the poems are often very mannered there are attempts here and there to s t a t e things simply, as in "Shadow":

> I saw her yesterday.
> And lo, there is no time
> Each second being eternity.

After a while the romance died down, but they remained friends. Hilda, who in those days attended Bryn

Mawr, later went to the University of Pennsylvania. According to Norman Holmes Pearson, of Yale, to whom Hilda Doolittle left her manuscripts and letters, she began to write poems in 1910 when, for a brief period, she was living in New York. These poems, she said, were modelled on Theocritus, whom she knew through a translation that Pound had given her. In 1910 she began to publish items in a New York syndicated newspaper and also wrote some stories and articles on astronomy for a Presbyterian paper, probably the Philadelphia *Sunday School Times*, to which she had been introduced by Homer Pound. Pearson believes that it was to be with Pound that she went to England in 1911. By that time he was making a name for himself in that country. He introduced her to London and was instrumental in having some of her verse published both there and in the United States. With her husband, the English poet Richard Aldington, she was a member, between 1912 and 1914, of Pound's Imagist group. In 1914 Pound separated from the group and it was taken over, with the approval of the other poets, by Amy Lowell. There was ill-feeling, and in 1915 Hilda wrote of "a beastly letter from E.P." — a letter to the poet F. S. Flint on Imagism; she advised Flint not to answer it. The storm passed, however, and she and Pound seem to have remained friends until her death in the 1960s.

Among Pound's other friends during his university years were several Wyncote residents, including the Rev. James Biddle Halsey, Vicar of All Hallows Episcopal Church at the corner of Greenwood Avenue and Bent Road, Wyncote. Pound sometimes played chess with him. Another friend was the painter Frank Reed Whiteside who lived in Washington Lane, Wyncote. Twenty years older than Pound, Whiteside studied first at the Pennsylvania Academy of Fine Arts and later in Paris. He spent some years in Wyncote, after his return from Europe, and then moved to Philadelphia. He was shot outside his Philadelphia home in 1929, but no one was ever charged with the crime.

Pound was friendly also with a young woman, Miss Adele Polk, who lived with her parents in Washington Lane.

He often visited her home and occasionally Miss Polk would call at the Pound home. A few years later he sent her an inscribed copy of *A Lume Spento*.

About 1905, when he was 20, Pound began to develop serious eye-trouble. He had worn glasses since the age of 5 or 6; as he grew older the eyes worsened. "At about twenty," he wrote in a letter to James Joyce in 1917, "I found that an inharmonic astigmatism was supposedly driving towards blindness (probably very remote) and also twisting my spine." In an effort to solve Joyce's eye-trouble Pound recommended him to try Dr George Milbry Gould of Philadelphia. He described how Gould had made a simple adjustment to his lenses: "suddenly felt 'a weight lifted,' and have had practically no bother since. The man who took me to Gould, himself a doctor, had had a much worse time, and felt he owed his eyesight to Gould and to the same simple means of correcting strain."

Gould, whose rooms during the 1890s were at 925 Walnut Street, Philadelphia, lived at 119 S. 17th Street; he was an ophthalmologist and writer on medical subjects, and was interested in what he believed was a connection between genius and eyestrain; he was also editor of *Gould's Medical Dictionary*, first published in 1904. By 1908 he was president of the American Medicine Publishing Company and lived at 1722 Walnut Street. When prevailed upon to give an opinion by mail on Joyce's condition Gould prescribed on-the-spot treatment in Zurich, where Joyce was then living. This course, in fact, had already been taken: Joyce's condition had deteriorated and in August 1917, before Gould's letter arrived, he had undergone surgery in Zurich.

Pound received his Master of Arts degree in June 1906 and about the same time was awarded the Harrison Fellowship in Romanics. This honour brought with it a salary of five hundred dollars and covered the period from September 1906 to the end of May 1907. As a result of this windfall he spent the summer of 1906 in Europe — this time on his own. Part of the holiday was taken up with study in preparation

57

for the thesis on Lope de Vega that he hoped to present in a year or two towards his doctorate. In Paris he went exploring with a young Frenchman Mathurin Dondo who was studying at the University of Pennsylvania. Dondo was a mild-mannered poet who at that time wrote verses in the style of Alfred de Musset; according to Pound later, he was regarded with suspicion by some of his classmates and was accused by Burtron Hessler of trying to corrupt America with his French ways. In the 1950s Dondo published *Histoire Naturel,* a book of poems written in a laconic modern manner which aroused Pound's admiration. In 1959 he described it as "one of the few books of contemporary French verse I can read with pleasure."

The *Hatboro Public Spirit* announced on June 2nd 1906: "Ezra Pound has gone abroad." According to the *Jenkintown Times-Chronicle* he was in Spain by the first week of June, or perhaps earlier, for on June 9th it carried this note: "Wyncote has been represented at Madrid, Spain, during the wedding of the young King, by Ezra, son of Homer L. Pound, who expects to be there several weeks." The paper reported on August 11th that he was home again. On his return he published two articles in the September 1906 issue of the *Book News Monthly,* run by the John Wanamaker store. One was called "Raphaelite Latin" and was devoted to the Latin poets of the Renaissance; the other was a review of two books about the troubadours which he had picked up in Paris. These were the first articles he ever published. In the October issue of the *Monthly* he gave an account of his recent visit to Burgos in Spain, under the title "Burgos, a Dream City of Old Castile."

In the autumn of 1906 he returned to the university to spend his year as Harrison Fellow. His studies included Provençal poetry and the *Chanson de Roland,* Dante's *Vita Nuova* and Lope de Vega's *Estrella de Sevilla.* In February 1907 while he was in the midst of his post-graduate studies, there occurred one of the most exciting events ever witnessed at Wyncote — the destruction by fire of the Wanamaker mansion "Lyndenhurst" and the rescue by local citizens of

John Wanamaker's Wyncote house, "Lyndenhurst".

The Wanamaker lake on which Pound and his friends skated.

JOHN WANAMAKER'S MANSION IN ASHES

Beautiful Lyndenhurst, His Country Home, Entirely Destroyed by Fire.

RARE PAINTINGS SAVED

"Christ Before Pilate" and "The Crucifixion" Carried Out Just in Time.

Special to "The Record."

Jenkintown, Pa., Feb. 8.—"Lyndenhurst," the magnificent country home of John Wanamaker, was completely ruined by fire this evening, and with all the expensive furnishings, except some of the larger and more valuable paintings, were destroyed. Half a dozen fire companies, some of them from Philadelphia, were powerless, owing to the freezing up of the water supply. The loss will certainly reach $1,500,000.

Mr. Wanamaker and his family are in Philadelphia during the winter, and the country house is in charge of a caretaker.

The estate covers more than 30 acres on the Old York road east of the line dividing Abington and Cheltenham townships. The grand mansion, partly English in architecture, was back about 350 yards from York road, and was reached by wide driveways.

The fire was first seen about 7 o'clock in the western wing of the building. The alarm was immediately telephoned to Jenkintown and to Ogontz; but the fire, supposed to have started from a crossed or defective electric light wire, had then made considerable headway.

The Pioneer and Independent Fire Companies from Jenkintown were first on the scene, their apparatus being dragged through the deep snow, or by trolley cars, for more than a mile.

The Old York Road Fire Company, of Elkins Park; the Ashbourne, of Ashburne, the two from Glenside, and the Branchtown, all the suburban companies, were also rushed to the scene.

WATER SUPPLY FROZEN.

Arrived there, they found the water supply frozen and the flames practically eating their way through the building, with nothing to be done for some time to stop the spread.

The frozen plugs were finally opened, and several streams were turned on the fire, together with the chemical service of the Old York Road Company; but the streams were as nothing in the roaring furnace, and all the several thousand spectators could do was to stand by and see the magnificent structure, with its treasured contents, speedily reduced to ashes and crumbling walls.

When it was seen that the building was doomed efforts were made to save many of the very valuable oil paintings in the art gallery of Lyndenhurst, and the best of the furniture and statuary. The firemen and the members of the police forces of Cheltenham and Jenkintown repeatedly made their way into the burning mansion, and at great risk amid falling glass and burning embers, pulled many of the more valuable paintings from the walls and carried furniture, statuary, bric-a-brac, cut glass and art treasures from the house, piling them indiscriminately in the 18 inches of snow on the Lyndhurst lawns. Many thousands of dollars' worth were saved in this manner; so the aggregate loss on the building and contents can only be approximated.

The water supply consisted only of the pressure forced from the pumping stations of the Wanamaker estate at Chelten Hills, and this was only moderate, compared with the pressing demands of the emergency.

A MOST IMPRESSIVE SPECTACLE.

The fire was a most spectacular one, and attracted thousands of persons from Jenkintown, Wycote, Ogontz, Abington, Elkins Park and Oak Lane. The glare lit up the skies for miles, and was equally visible in the northern parts of Philadelphia.

Many suburbanites in dinner and theatre attire gave up their engagements and rushed to the fire, standing in the snow until the work of destruction was completed.

At 9 o'clock the fire was at its height, the flames pouring from every lofty tower and window and making a glare by which a newspaper could be read half a mile away. Chief Saddington, of Cheltenham, detailed men to guard the paintings and art objects saved, and these officers were aided by Officers Sheehan and Kelly from Jenkintown.

The Philadelphia delegation of firemen arrived too late to have been of much assistance, even if there had been an adequate and available water supply. They came under the direction of Assistant Engineer Charles Waters, on the Reading-Lehigh Valley Buffalo express, which left the Reading Terminal at 8.40, and had orders to stop at Chelten Hills.

GRAND PAINTINGS RESCUED.

Difficult as was the work of the firemen, they were able to prevent the consuming flames reaching the fine stables adjoining the mansion. Four men, at the risk of their lives, realizing that the house itself was doomed to utter destruction, then rushed into the fiery building and cut from the main wall of the art gallery two of the rarest paintings, Munkacsy's "Christ Before Pilate" and "The Crucifixion." These two great works of art alone are valued at $150,000. The art rescuers, Dr. J.

Continued on Fifth Page.

John Wanamaker's Mansion in Ashes

Continued From First Page.

Frederick Herbert, of Ogontz: Louis R. Dutton, of Jenkintown: Homer L. Pound and J. Shrider, of Wyncote, carried these mammoth paintings to the larger barn and guarded them there. A little later Mr. McLeod, Mr. Wanamaker's son-in-law, arrived, and had the paintings removed to one of the adjacent bungalows, where they are still under guard.

Many other works of art of lesser value, and magnificent specimens of furniture and ornamentation, were saved from the destroyed mansion, and nearly the entire great collection in the art galleries might have been carried out if the first neighbors and firemen to arrive had known how sweeping and disastrous the fire was destined to be, in view of the critical shortage of water.

The firemen are still playing streams upon the ruins.

MAID FAILS TO TURN OFF CURRENT.

It appears that the flames were discovered at a quarter past 6 o'clock. A maid who had been ironing in the linen room had, on going out, failed to turn off the electric current, and the iron became so hot that it set fire to the woodwork. Alexander Tait, one of the watchmen about the premises, discovered the blaze, and the servants tried to extinguish it, and, finding this impossible, the fire company at Jenkintown was telephoned for, as well as those of the other near-by places. Mr. Wanamaker, who was at his Walnut street residence, in the city, was then notified, and he instructed them to save the pictures above all else, particularly the two by Munkacsy. Redman Wanamaker, who was at the city home with Norman McLeod, took the first train to Jenkintown, and upon arriving took charge of removing the furnishings and placing them in safety. All hope of saving the great mansion had then been abandoned.

It was two hours and a half before the art galleries caught fire. They were separate from the house and protected by a fire-proof wall, but when the roof of the main building came crashing down the sparks and heat started them burning.

Then the effort was made to save the pictures. The Munkacsys were so large that the canvases had to be cut from the frames, carefully rolled and then laid away. With the exception of these large pictures all of the others were taken down, frames and all. Some were placed in the carriage house and others merely stood against trees in the snow and covered with rugs and tapestries.

There was an attempt to remove a grand piano; but a slip and a fall, and the beautiful instrument went down with a crash.

Mr. Wanamaker, after being assured that the more valuable paintings were saved, went to bed at his city home while the fire was still raging.

The loss in actual money value cannot be compared to the destruction of the treasures to which a deep sentimental value attached. One of these valued collections was Mr. Wanamaker's Americana library, consisting of several thousand books, rare old editions which have no duplicates and cost as much as $1000 apiece. They had been gathered from all parts of the world, and the collection had taken a lifetime.

Everything that Mrs. Wanamaker owned was in the house. Her collection of china, which was of great value; her silver, which was even more costly; furniture, antiques and other articles that cannot be replaced. One rug in the library was valued at $30,000, and tapestries of almost priceless worth went to feed the hungry and all-devouring flames.

Next morning's newspaper account of Wanamaker fire of February 8th 1907.

"Lyndenhurst" after the fire.

many of its art works. According to Pound, who was present, it was like a scene from the French Revolution.

The fire broke out about six o'clock in the evening of Friday February 8th when a servant apparently forgot to turn off an electric iron and left it on an ironing-board in the linen-room. Adele Polk, who was attending a birthday party at the home of Dr. W. A. Cross, said in 1969 they heard the fire-sirens about half past six. Sensing something on a grand scale residents of Wyncote, Chelten Hills and other nearby villages and townships rushed to the scene. In the words of the *Philadelphia Evening Bulletin* of the following day February 9th, "crowds began to come from all directions — in trolley-cars, in automobiles, and in closed carriages. Women wrapped up in furs, sat down in chairs that had been carried out of the house and deposited on the snow." Around the blazing mansion there "was a gigantic circle of furniture, tapestries, rugs, pictures — and people." Finally the crowd became so large that a force of fifty policemen was sent for, to guard the objects rescued from the edifice.

A number of local residents, including Homer and Ezra Pound, rushed into the burning building to help rescue the paintings and other works of art in danger. Here is the *Evening Bulletin's* description of the rescue:

> It was two hours and a half before the art galleries caught. They were separate from the house and protected by a fireproof wall, but when the roof of the main building came crashing down, sending up clouds of sparks and tongues of flame, the heat became so intense that the galleries began to burn.
>
> Then a party, headed by Homer L. Pound and J. W. Hunsberger of Wyncote, started in to save the pictures. The Munkacsys were too large to be carried out in their frames — they are each about twenty feet square — so the canvases were cut with a sharp knife, close to the woodwork, rolled up carefully and carried into the carriage house.

All the smaller pictures were taken from the walls, frames and all. Some of them were put into the carriage house, and some were merely stood up in the snow against trees. They were covered with rugs and tapestries to prevent the heat from cracking them.

Ezra, who helped to carry some of these paintings to safety, said later he thought they "were all fakes." He and a friend also attempted to carry out a grand piano. They got it as far as the stairs, after which it travelled swiftly of its own accord. There was little left intact when it hit the bottom. Among the large paintings saved by Homer was the Munkacsy "Crucifixion" still to be seen at Wanamaker's store in Philadelphia. At the time of the the fire the total loss, including the house, paintings, rare books, antiques, etc., was estimated at $1,500,000. Shortly after the fire Mr John Wanamaker sent formal "thank you" letters to the townsfolk for their assistance.

It was probably about this time that Pound published some of his prose pieces signed E. P., in a periodical pamphlet called *The Half Hour* which was printed at the author's (or perhaps his father's) expense. It was small (about 4 by 3 inches) and contained few pages. There was only one issue.

III

When in 1907 his Harrison Fellowship was not renewed for a further year Pound decided to leave the University of Pennsylvania without completing his doctorate. It was during the summer of 1907 while he was looking for a teaching job that he went to Scudders Falls (just north of Trenton, New Jersey) to the country home of a young man by the name of John Scudder who needed some tutoring in French, and perhaps other languages, in order to get into college. One day while Pound was lying in a hammock on the porch of the farmhouse John Scudder drove up in a buggy, accompanied by a young woman. Only Pound's bushy hair was visible. "Who is that curly mop?" the young woman asked, and Scudder replied: "That's the chap who is trying to get me in college." Later that evening Pound met the young woman at dinner. Her name was Mary S. Moore and she lived at 136 West State Street, Trenton — a large stone townhouse directly opposite the New Jersey State House. (In a letter to Miss Moore a few months later, Pound referred to the house's fine architecture and "exact colonial doorway.") Her father, Henry C. Moore, was Vice-President of the Trenton Street Railway and later President of the Broad Street Bank in Trenton. Another member of the family, Edward J. Moore, was a banker in Philadelphia. Miss Moore had attended the Model School on North Clinton Street, Trenton. She and Pound were immediately attracted to one another and their romance continued for some time. She paid a number of visits to the Scudder farmhouse and Ezra called at her home in Trenton. Later, Miss Moore visited 166 Fernbrook Avenue and met Homer and Isabel Pound. With Trenton and Wyncote connected by the Reading Railroad they saw a good deal of one another. Among the letters he wrote her at this time is one saying that if John Scudder and his father went off to the coast as planned, he would visit her immediately in Trenton. In another (probably written on Sunday, June 27th 1907) he addressed her as "Dear Santa Teresa" and went on:

> Forgive us our "stupidities." And if it please thee lunch with us (i.e. me) at Wanamaker's Tea Rooms — or where thou wilt — when *en route* to Richmond.
>
> The gods avail thee.
>
> By the way, such of my affairs as I mentioned yesterday were for your gracious ears alone, as you perhaps surmised.

He also addressed her, in other letters, as "Miss Mary Moore," "Delectable Rabbit," "Maridhu," "Your Ladyship," "Grey Eyes," and "Most beloved absurdity." Writing on August 27th or 28th at Wyncote he wondered whether it would be best to send her manuscripts of some of his poems or wait until he could "make a book" for her. He said he had been trying "to bluff" the authorities at Williams College (Williamstown, Mass.) into exempting John Scudder from his French exam. He alluded to a new job: "And also the local paper states that I have gone to Indiana which shows extraordinary tho' not unprecedented foresight on the part of the local eyes." On September 1st he wrote: "That show party will have to be on Wednesday Sept. eleventh if it is at all — because there will only be you and Hilda and the auto [?] Kid and me."

In the autumn of 1907 Pound took up a teaching post (French, Spanish, Italian) at Wabash College, Crawfordsville, Indiana. By this time he seems to have been thinking of marriage, for in a letter to Miss Moore from the Crawford Hotel, Crawfordsville, he informed her that he had no intention of fitting up a place that would not be convertible into a dwelling for two. He supposed that they would want something "semi-sylvan" but not too far from the heart of things. Writing from Milligan Terrace, Crawfordsville, he wondered what her "grey eyes" would make of its gothic-style architecture — eyes that were used to the gracious doorway of her own home in Trenton, a late Federal house built about 1810. "I went out and inspected just now," he told her, "and somehow I am not at all afraid that you will be disappointed when I bring you here." He would be sending her some poems, but others would mean more, he thought, if read to her by their author who knew their imperfections and could supply by tone what was missing from the words. One of the poems he sent ("to be read with due gravity even as I made it") included these lines:

> I lay on my back and stretched
> > I layed my books aside
> And beheld the leaves, wind-caught-un-furled
> Showing their reverse sides.
> And a little cloud looked at me
> > From around the trees trunk beside me
> And winked
> And I knew that it was well with the world . . .

Another poem read:

> Always the spirit within
> Shaping the form without
>
> Wind being upon the grass made the
> > sun-sheen quiver
> And unsettled the shadows.

Some of his letters to her were practical: in one he bemoaned the fact that only poor quality cigarettes were available in Crawfordsville and asked her to send some "real cigarettes." When they arrived he told her she was a very nice "rabbit-kitten," even if she had made the mistake of addressing them to Crawfordsville, *Pennsylvania!* At one

Adele Polk photographed February 1907 by her brother James in backyard of Polk house, Washington Lane, Wyncote. Writing to Carl Gatter on January 5th 1957 Pound wondered that she had never married: "Mebbe she was choosey. I think there was English ancestry. Blimey, was her paw a bit fussy??"

Autumnus

(An Autistave on Earnest Dowson's)
"Spring of the Soul" (?)

Lo! that the wood standeth drearily!
But gaunt great banners staweth the trees
Have lost their sun-shot summer panoplies,
& only the weeping pines are green,
— the pines that weep for a whole world's teen.
Yet the Spring of the Soul.. the Spring of the Soul
Claimeth its own in thee & me.

Lo! the world waggeth wearily,
As gaunt grey shadows its people be
Taking life's burthen drearily.
Yet each hath some hidden joy I ween.
Should each one tell where his dream
hath been
The Spring of the Soul, the Spring of the Soul
Might claim more vassals
than
me & thee.

E.P.

Pound poem in holograph, c. 1907. (Yale Univ. Library)

Mary Moore of Trenton, N.J.,
c. 1910, when she was about 25.

The Moore house, 136 West
State St., Trenton, opposite New
Jersey State House. Built about
1810 it was sometimes used by
the legislature when the State
House was undergoing repairs.
It was demolished in 1932.

PIANOFORTE SOLI ·   ·   ·   Toccata in G major ·   ·   · *Bach*

                    Sonata, Op. 78 ·   ·   · *Beethoven*

Adagio cantabile—Allegro ma non troppo—Allegro vivace.

           " Reflets dans l'eau " }
            Prelude   } ·   · *Debussy*

Miss ELSIE HALL.

SONGS ·   ·   ·   (*a*)   Clair de Lune ·   ·   · *Gabriel Fauré*

                      (*b*)   Lied Maritime ·   ·   · *Vincent d'Indy*

                      (*c*)   " Ariettes Oubliées ' (No. 3) ·   · *Debussy*

                      (*d*)   " Aquarelles " (Green) ·   · *Debussy*

                      (*e*)   " Fêtes Galantes "—Fantoches ·   · *Debussy*

Miss FLORENCE SCHMIDT.

CLAIR DE LUNE.

Votre âme est un paysage choisi
Que vont charmant masques et bergamasques
Jouant du luth et dansant, et quasi
Tristes, sous leurs déguisements fantasques !

Tout en chantant sur le mode mineur,
L'amour vainqueur et la vie opportune ;
Ils n'ont pas l'air de croire à leur bonheur,
Et leur chanson se mêle au clair de lune !

Au calme clair de lune, triste et beau,
Qui fait rêver les oiseaux dans les arbres,
Et sangloter d'extase les jets d'eau,
Les grands jets d'eau sveltes parmi les marbres !

                    Paul Verlaine.

English Version.

Your soul is a country chosen,
Befit for maskings, and folk galliard-clad
To touch the luth and dance in,
Yet be beneath their masks a little sad.

Where all shall sing in minor melody
That love is vanquisher, and life-chance's spoils
among,
Yet seem mistrustful of their fortune there,
Where moonlight tangles in the web of song.

The calm clear of the moon so sad, so fair,
Doth snare the birds within its net of dreams.
And mid the marbles where the water-jets
Sob for the rapture in their pale, tall streams.

                    Ezra Pound.

LIED MARITIME.

Au loin, dans la mer, s'éteint le soleil,
Et la mer est calme et sans ride ;
Le flot diapré s'étale sans bruit,
Caressant la grève assombrie.
Tes yeux, tes traitres yeux, sont clos,
Et mon cœur est tranquille comme la mer.

Au loin, sur la mer, l'orage est levé,
Et la mer s'émeut et bouillonne ;
Le flot, jusqu'aux cieux, s'érige superbe,
Et croule en hurlant vers les abimes.
Tes yeux, tes traitres yeux si doux,
Me regardent jusqu'au fond de l'âme,
Et mon cœur torturé, mon cœur bienheureux,
S'exalte et se brise comme la mer.

English Version.

Fadeth the sun on the sea afar,
The calm, unrippled sea ;
Jasper wave falls silently
To touch the o'ershadowed shore.
Thine eyes, thy traitorous eyes, are closed ;
Tranquil my heart so, as the sea is still.

Riseth the storm on the sea afar,
With moving rage of the sea ;
Rise waves towards heaven mightily,
And wail to their deep troughs clamorous.
Thine eyes, thy traitorous eyes, look down
Into the wave-troughs of my soul,
Till my heart, tortured, doth exalt himself,
And break as gainst the rocks some mighty
sea.

                    Ezra Pound.

From Mrs Derwent Wood's concert programme of March 1910 ; translations by Pound.

Bride Scratton

Dorothy Pound

stage they appear to have become engaged, and because he did not think he would be able to find a suitable ring in Crawfordsville he sent her one that had been given him in Philadelphia by the pianist Katherine Ruth Heyman. In signing the letter which accompanied the ring he wrote, "I love you, Ezra."

In another letter about this time he insisted that she would be going abroad with him the following summer. "We need spend no futile time in disputing the matter." Soon, however, Miss Moore wrote to say that she was engaged to a man by the name of Oscar MacPherson. In one of his replies he said: "You see I have the trick of being serious only at inconvenient times." In another: "I trusted in a dream — having learned to trust mine own dreams, I trusted another's — presumed." Here is one of his final letters to her from Indiana:

Dear Furry Little Rabbit:

I do not love you at all except as I love all beautiful things that run around in the sunlight and are happy.

As soon as my Mat Arnoldesque high serious-ness invaded my letters you abandoned me. Got engaged to Oscar. Besides the plumbing in Craw-fordsville is beneath your exquisiteness.

You don't like geniuses. I'm sorry but they are nice toys at times.

Miss Moore did not marry Oscar MacPherson, but some years later, another by the name of Frederick Cross. When in 1909 Pound published in London a collection of poems entitled *Personae* he dedicated it as follows:

This Book Is For
MARY MOORE
Of Trenton, If She
Wants It

When a presentation copy arrived from the author in London Miss Moore read through the poems but did not, apparently, see the dedication. It was several months before someone pointed out to her that it was dedicated to "Mary Moore of Trenton," with an additional note in the poet's own hand:

In attestation whereof I
do set and sign

EP

Pound and Miss Moore remained friends. She met him in London in 1912, when he showed her some of the sights, and again in Rapallo during the winter of 1931-2. She in the meantime had become Mrs. Cross. He continued to write to her after the Second World War.

IV

Before the end of 1907 Pound discovered that he did not like Wabash College. Nor did the college like him. He was too much of a bohemian with a taste for the company of theatrical folk and artists. He was even caught serving breakfast coffee to a stranded female of the theatrical species. Early in 1908 he and the college arrived at a solution considered satisfactory by both parties. He gave up his job and the college agreed to give him the rest of his year's salary. Unable to find a publisher for his first collection of poems and feeling that there was nothing left for him in the United States he sailed for Spain and Italy in February 1908. His final article before he left was a piece entitled "M. Antonius Flaminius and John Keats, A Kinship in Genius," which was published in the February issue of the *Book News Monthly*. In sailing for Europe he was setting forth on a journey through many cultures and countries; never again would he call Wyncote home. Just before he left, a citizen of Philadelphia, William B. Smith (not to be confused with William Brooke Smith) did Pound a favour which a year later helped him make his way in London. Smith was a travel agent at 900 Chestnut Street; his home was at 700 North Franklin Street. In a note written in Venice in May 1968, for a reprint of his book *The Spirit of Romance,* Pound remembered him thus:

> A fellow named Smith put me on the road which led to the publication of this book — my first published prose work. He was a Philadelphia

travel agent whom I had first seen as a boy, in 1898, when my great-aunt Frank had taken us on a grand tour of Europe. I recognized him again by a peculiar movement of his left arm, the elbow had been badly reset, while I was getting off to Europe on my own, after Crawfordsville. With my ticket he gave me a note to a man in London named Sullivan who had something to do with Covent Garden Market. I do not know how, but he persuaded the London Polytechnic to let me give a course of lectures there.

These lectures, derived from a seminar conducted by Rennert, were worked up into a book and published in 1910 as *The Spirit of Romance*. At the end of his 1968 note Pound dedicated the reprint "to 'Smith' with thanks."

During his stay of some months in Venice in 1908, Pound became manager for the concert pianist, Katherine Ruth Heyman, a friend from Philadelphia. Through his energy as publicist a story appeared in the *Gazzetta di Venezia* of July 28th 1908, under the heading, "Katherine Roth Heymann Concert in the Liceo Marcello Hall." And continued: "Yesterday evening Miss Katherine Roth Heymann, a very gracious American brunette from Philadelphia, who studied in Berlin, gave a concert in the Benedetto Marcello hall." The concert was for invited guests only, the story explained, and the invitations were distributed with "great parsimony." The audience was restricted but "intellectual and refined," composed largely of foreigners and students of music. She played Chopin, Liszt, Scarlatti, Moskowsky, etc. The paper praised her precision. "She may return for a public concert in the Winter."

The *Book News Monthly* of Philadelphia continued to take an interest in Pound's work during his first year or two abroad. After the appearance of his first book *A Lume Spento* it carried a note in which his talent was praised and a forceful future anticipated. In 1909 Curtis Hidden Page reviewed *A Lume Spento* and *Personae* at some length:

The most original note struck in English verse, since the publication of Ernest Dowson's poems some three or four years ago, rings through the songs and dramatic lyrics of two volumes, partly identical with each other, by Ezra Pound . . . The first impression one receives from them is that their author has gone a little mad from overmuch reading of Browning, Morris, Yeats, Verlaine, Mallarmé, Symons, Dowson, and even the American poets of Vagabondia, Hovey and Carman . . . On closer knowledge, and after sympathetic rereading, he proves to be mad only after Hamlet's fashion; and to be speaking dramatically, with a manner wholly his own, if not wholly new . . . This poet, in spite of frequent roughness (often intentional), is a true singer, genuinely carrying on the tradition of the schools of Henley, Symons, Hovey, Dowson — and Browning; a strange combination, but truly representing the literary spirit of today.

In London in 1909 Pound began mixing in the city's various literary circles. He cultivated some of the established writers as well as the "modernistic" young. The well-known essayist and poet, Alice Meynell, for example, gave him a copy of her book *Ceres' Runaways and other essays* (London 1909), with the following inscription: "Ezra Pound with all the author's good wishes September 7th 1909." And in February 1910 Mrs Derwent Wood asked him to provide English translations of a group of French and Italian songs that she sang, under her maiden name Florence Schmidt, in a concert at the Bechstein Hall, London, on March 1st. Another of his friends at this time was Bride Scratton, a married woman a few years older than Pound, whom he had met at a literary evening at William Butler Yeats's flat in Woburn Buildings. It may have been her photograph that William Carlos Williams saw, when, in March 1910, after postgraduate study in Germany, he visited Pound in London. The photograph was on Pound's dresser, with a candle burning before it. When Bride Scratton was divorced by her husband in 1923 Pound was named as co-respondent.

After becoming something of a success in London Pound returned to the United States for a visit in 1910. His parents had let the Wyncote house and were living in Philadelphia, with a short period, during the second half of 1910, at Swarthmore. Pound spent much of his time in New York where on August 11th he met the artist John Sloan at the Petipas restaurant. In his diary Sloan wrote: "Mr Pound the poet was with Mr King. I was interested in him, he studied at the U. of P. in Phila. and knows Frank Whiteside and Breckenridge. From what I have heard he is a 'very good' poet." Hugh Henry Breckenridge (b. 1870) was an artist who lived a good part of his life in Philadelphia; he was a friend of Whiteside. Sloan's diary entry for August 13th reads: "At 3 o'clock Mr Yeats [W. B. Yeats's father] came and he and Dolly and I went down town. Met John Quinn [New York lawyer and patron of the arts] and Mr King and Mr Pound at the World Building and as Mr Quinn's guests we saw Coney Island."

On November 8th 1910 Pound dined with a family called Del Mar, who were friends of an American hostess, Mrs Alfred Fowler, whom he had met in London. Mrs Fowler's husband, "Taffy," is mentioned in canto 18 and again in later cantos. It would be interesting to know if these Del Mars were related to the 19th century American historian, Alexander Del Mar, whose work Pound began to insert into his cantos some forty years later.

By January 1911 Pound was staying with his parents at 1834 Mt. Vernon Street, Philadelphia. His first book of poems in America, *Provença*, came out in November 1910; on January 6th 1911 the American critic Floyd Dell discussed Pound at length in the "Friday Literary Review" of the *Chicago Evening Post*. He called him " a very new kind of poet," of "shocking vigour," who was capable of creating "art of a high order." This obviously pleased Pound, for on January 20th he wrote Dell a letter, giving the Mt. Vernon Street house as his address: "I feel almost as if I should apologize for my naive surprising at finding a critic who has considered both the function of criticism and the nature of the book before him." He went on to discuss some of the "influences" which Dell had discovered in his poetry. He admitted that he had followed Browning in *Personae,* and then went on: "Whitman? I never have owned a copy of Whitman, I have to all purposes never read him. What you and everyone else take for Whitman is *America.* The feel of the air, the geomorphic rhythm force." Later in the letter he remarked, "don't mind my rambling — I'm just out of hospital and not having had a pen in my hands for some time it burbles." He ended with these words: "This note seems to presuppose an ungodly amount of interest on your part, but I've only found one man to whom I can talk, or at whom I can theorize, or what you will, since I landed seven months ago, & voilà, you get the effects."[1] Pound left New York for Europe in February 1911 and did not return again until 1939.

During his years in England and on the Continent the Philadelphia newspapers often carried stories about his progress as a poet and critic. Thus in the summer of 1911 when he went to stay at Sirmione, on Lake Garda, Italy, the *Evening Bulletin* ran a long story about his travels and publications. Of his recent work it said: "Now another volume, the *Canzoni of Ezra Pound* is on the verge of publication in London and will shortly be issued. Early proofs of these songs have been sent by Mr Pound to his father, Homer Loomis Pound, who lives at 1834 Mount Vernon Street, and is assistant assayer in the United States Mint, 17th and Spring Garden Streets." The Mount Vernon Street house was a large fashionable townhouse which the Pounds rented during 1911. In 1912 they took a similar house at 1640 Green Street, Philadelphia, before returning to Wyncote.

Living abroad Pound did not forget the poetry of his University of Pennsylvania friend William Carlos Williams, who was by now a full-fledged doctor in New Jersey. In 1912 he persuaded the editor of the London *Poetry Review*

[1] Quotations from G. Thomas Tanselle, "Two Early Letters of Ezra Pound," *American Literature* (March 1972).

The painter Frank Reed Whiteside of Washington Lane, Wyncote.
Pastel by Hugh Breckenridge.

PHILADELPHIA POET HAILED IN ENGLAND

Ezra Pound, Although But 24 Years Old, Has Won Great Reputation With His Verse Abroad

PARENTS LIVE IN THIS CITY

Few Philadelphians—even those of the innermost literary circle—are aware that they can claim citizenship with Ezra Pound, the young American poet, who has been "discovered" in England.

Few, indeed, know that this young man, who has captured the critics as well as the literary craftsmen in England and the Continent, has spent almost his entire life in this city, where he received his education and won honors as a student at the University of Pennsylvania.

Although, like the young Lochinvar, Ezra Pound "came out of the West," his home is at 1834 Mount Vernon st., where his parents, Mr. and Mrs. Homer L. Found, now reside. His father, who is assistant assayer at the United States Mint, 17th and Spring Garden sts., is a son of Thaddeus E. Pound, former Governor of Wisconsin. On his mother's side he is distantly related to Longfellow.

The path of poesy which Ezra Pound chose in his boyhood is somewhat beset with difficulties here in America, but the youthful poet—he is only twenty-four years old—is undaunted. He has set his goal high.

"I want to write before I die the greatest poems that have ever been written," he told his parents in outlining his life work as a lad.

And he is on his way toward his goal, if the opinions of the most competent critics count for anything. His career thus far, though it has really but just started, gives the lie to the belief so often expressed that no one nowadays can succeed in having his poetic work published without having sufficient money to guarantee such publication. Pound went to England with just about enough cash to pay for board and lodging and was almost instantly successful in getting a hearing.

The best evidence of this is the fact that he is now delivering a course of lectures on "Mediaeval Literature" at the London Polytechnic—no mean honor in itself. He has published only four small books of verse, "Exultations," "Personae," "A Lume Spento," or "With Tapers Quenched," and "A Quinzaine for this Yule," but this is no indication that he is indolent, barren or slow in achieve-

EZRA POUND,
A Philadelphian bred, a University of Pennsylvania man, who is being hailed in England as a remarkable poet, and seemingly one destined to write great verse. Mr. Pound is only twenty-four years old. His father is employed at the United States Mint here, and lives on Mt. Vernon st.
(Photograph by Elliott & Fry.)

ment. He has a faculty for self-criticism and has written and destroyed two novels and some 300 sonnets. He has also just completed a prose work entitled "The Spirit of Romance," a history of romance and literature which is being published in London, and it is expected will shortly be brought out in this country.

London "Punch" has voiced Pound's claim to attention in the following remarkable judgment:

"He has succeeded where all others have failed in evolving a blend of the imagery of the unfettered West, the vocabulary of Wardour Street and the sinister abandon of Borgiac Italy. His verse is the most remarkable thing in poetry since Robert Browning."

His work shows individuality, passion, force; it abounds in mysticism, archaic words and unfamiliar metres that baffle the reader. For Pound scorns the limitations of form and metre and suits his expression to the mood with a surpassingly beautiful result that combines fierceness, tenderness and virility. One of his best known poems, a ballad that awoke widespread interst in this country as well as in England, is his "Ballad of the Goodly Fere." It purports to be a speech made some time after the Crucifixion by Simon Zelotes, one of the least among the Twelve Apostles. Simon was a poor fisherman and the poet attempts to give expression in Simon's words to the ____ ____ ____ at the passing of ____ "goodly fere." Fere is the old Anglo-Saxon word meaning mate or companion.

The Evening Bulletin, Philadelphia, December 2nd 1909.

Poet Who Will Wed

POET IN LOVE SONG EXTOLS HIS BRIDE

Ezra Pound, Wyncote Boy, Who Achieved Fame Abroad, Soon to Wed.

(Photo by Haeseler.)

Ezra Pound is a young man who went from Wyncote to England and there wrote poems of so much merit that he gained a special place in the highest literary circles. One of his writings led to a romance, a result of which is the announcement of his engagement to Miss Dorothy Shakespear, of London.

Phila. Poet in Stanza Tells of His Romance

Man's love follows many faces,
My love only one face knoweth;
Towards thee only my love
    floweth,
And outstrips the swift stream's
    paces.
Were this love well here dis-
    played,
    As flame flameth 'neath thin
    jade,
Love should glow through these,
    phrases.

Cable announcement of the coming marriage of Ezra Pound, the brilliant young Philadelphia poet, and Miss Dorothy Shakespear, daughter of Mr. and Mrs. Hope Shakespear, of London, the event to take place on Saturday April 18, and not on April 14, as first published, has attracted attention to the brilliant career of this youth, whose early days were spent at Wyncote, in the Old York Road section.

Pound has been haled in England as one of the world's great poets. Kipling has placed such an estimate on him, saying also that the young man's lyrical gifts are of the highest.

His romance has spurred the young author's Pegasus. It is sung in a canson, of which the stanza leading this article is a part. The poem is dedicated to Miss Shakespear and to her mother, Olivia Shakespear. Miss Shakespear's parents, live in Brunswick Gardens, London, where the marriage will be solemnized. She is just past twenty. The romance spans several years.

Mother Proud of Poet.

Pound's parents are Mr. and Mrs. Homer L. Pound, whose home is at 166 Fernbrook Avenue, Wyncote. The young man's mother is naturally very proud of her son's career, and yesterday talked entertainingly of his life abroad.

The Philadephia Press, March 26th 1914.

82

Ezra Pound's Father Tells How Son Went To London With a Shilling and Found Fame

U. S. Mint Assayer Here Discloses Famous Poet's Background and Brings to Light Simple Song He Wrote When First Facing the World

BY MARY DIXON THAYER.

Dawn Song

God hath put me here
In earth's goodly , here
   To sing the song of the day,
A strong, glad song,
If the road be long,
   To my fellows in the way.

So I make my song of the good,
   glad light
   That falls from the gate of the
     sun,
And the clear, cool wind that
     bloweth good
   To my brother, everyone.
         —Ezra Pound.

NOT since the days of "Dick" Whittington, perhaps, has a youth with only a shilling in his pocket gone up to London Town and won fame as quickly and unexpectedly as did a young Philadelphian, Ezra Pound.

The prize sum of $2,000 awarded Ezra Pound by the Dial recently, attracted attention once more to this poet, who is now living in Rapello, Genoa, but who hails from Philadelphia, and a graduate of the University of Pennsylvania. Ezra Pound's parents still are at Wyncote, and his father is assayer at the United States Mint here. 16th and Spring Garden sts.

It was there we found him, a tall, courtly, elderly gentleman, with white hair and a kindly manner.

It would be interesting if it were always possible to grant the "public" glimpse behind the scenes of fame, seek out those persons who have had the most influence in the lives of famous men and women, and to manifest, if only dimly and in part, the great truth that we are—all of us—that we are not through our own efforts or our own gifts alone, but by reason also of the influence and encouragement of others.

Thus it is that, talking with Ezra Pound's father, one suddenly becomes aware that this humble, old-world gen-

Always Had Nerve," He Says of Author of "Cantos" Who Found a Wife After "Crashing" Teaching Staff of London Polytechnic School

tleman, who tells you not to mention him in the article about his famous son because, after all, "nobody is interested in me," is in reality every bit as interesting as the poet himself. One finds oneself wondering, indeed, whether Ezra Pound would ever have achieved the laurels he has achieved but for his father's unfailing interest and understanding.

Likes to Talk About Ezra

"I like to talk about Ezra," said Mr. Pound, smiling, as we sat in his large private office at the Mint. "I got a letter from him this morning and here's a photo of my little grandson too. He's just fourteen months old and his name is Omar, after the famous poet, you know. Ezra says he wants to keep up the poetic tradition in the family. But here's Ezra's letter. Maybe you'd like to read it?"

Dear Dad: (we read) Enclosed teleg. from Monsieur Coogan. Also clip. from Paris Chi. Trib.

Article on part of Guido is due in March Dial. Various other matters suspended. Mail don't seem to arrive.

Hughes, as I think I said, is printing the Ta Hio, 20 copies of which shd. reach you, in, I spose six months time.

Am looking at empty apartments here, for you, whenever I see sign "To Let." Wot ells!

Kitty Heyman having success with Scriabine concerts in Paris.

Olga stopping off at Sta Margherita, goes on to Paris tomorrow.

Cournos in hospital in Switzerland. Contribution for Exile recd. from him this a. m.

Orrick Johns in Firenze. Haven't seen him. He was in hospital in Sicily last winter, then instead of coming here had to go to France to buy a new wooden leg.

Bill Bird talks of restarting his press. I return at last the photo, found in book trunk. Have you any idea who it is? Dem—d if I have. Nation been sitting on an article of mine fer months.

Love to you and mother,
         Ezra.

We copy the letter exactly as written because, for those who know Ezra Pound through his writings, it is so characteristic, even to the abbreviations.

"That's the way he always writes,' said Mr. Pound, "short, terse sentences. We hear from him often. What? Oh. yes, I know what he means by 'Wot ells,' but that's just between us two. We have lots of little secrets. The Ta Hio manuscript he mentions is his new translation of Confucius, and 'John Cournos' used to be a newspaper man here in Philadelphia, and 'Olga' is Olga Rudge, the famous violinist who plays with Anthiell. And Bill Bird published his first Cantos. And the telegram was from Jackie Coogan. And the photo is one I found in his old trunk full of manuscripts he wrote when he was at school and college. I've kept everything he's ever written, I guess. Ezra gets mad about it. 'For heaven's sake, Dad,' he writes every now and then, 'won't you get busy and burn up all that truck of mine you've got littering up your house? I'm afraid some of it will get into print some day, if you don't!'"

Mr. Pound laughed. "Maybe it will," he said, "and between you and me, I wouldn't mind, because I think some of the best stuff Ezra ever wrote was written when he was a young man. Anyhow, I can understand those writings of his better than some of his later ones. Have you read any of his Cantos?" he asked, quizzically. "Well, I must admit I can't make much out of some of them. Ezra told me unless I read Browning's 'Sordello' I couldn't expect to understand the Cantos.' So I waded through that. Ever read it? Well, I don't advise you to. I found it didn't help me much with Ezra's Cantos, anyway.

Discloses Old Poem of Son

"Ezra would just about kill me," said Mr. Pound, chuckling, "if he knew I was showing anybody this poem of his I came across yesterday among his old manuscripts. But it sort of appeals to me. Of course, it isn't poetry, really, but then, it wasn't meant to be. It's just nice and human, I think, and I remember so well when he wrote it. He had just come home from getting his diploma at the University and I remember he flung the diploma into a corner and shouted 'Well, Dad! Educated! And I said, 'What are your plans now, son? You've got to get busy and do something now, you know.' And with that he went off upstairs to his room, and came down a few minutes later with this poem. It's never been published except in a small-town paper out in Idaho, and as I said before Ezra would just about kill me if he knew I was

showing it to anybody. But it's sort of nice, I think. The sheet of yellowed paper read:

The Mourn of Life

There comes a time in the lives of men
That makes their blood turn cold
When their fathers say
In a gentle way
"Thou canst not stay
Any more in the dear home fold."

'Twill come some time to you,
When your noble Dad
Your loving Dad
Your dear Dad kind and true,
Will no more pay
In that generous way
Your bills as he used to do.

But will gently say
In his old, sweet way
Though the tone may ring some cool,
"I paid the stake
The dem—d high stake
While you loafed 'round school.

While you rushed the can
And played the man
A-smokin' your fine cheroots,.
I had to pay
In a hefty way
For a coon to black your boots.

Now, you're a Master of Arts,
And a man of parts,
Go forth, get on the job!"
There comes a time-in the lives of men
That makes their blood turn cool.
For the world is a place they've glanced
    upon
From ethereal heights afar,
Where each has fussed his chorus girl,
And each has dined his star.
And each has spent
What Dad has sent,
In ways a bit bizarre.

So go, little verse,
Go forth and be dem—d'
Throughout your limited sphere;
But prithee tell
To the bards in Hell
Who live on nothing a year,
That a Master of Arts
And a man of parts
Is trying the same thing here;

"Sort of human, isn't it?" said Mr. Pound, "that's just the way Ezra always was, and still is, even if he does write Cantos now that I don't catch onto exactly. Well, he went abroad shortly after that and when he'd spent every cent he'd saved out of his allowance, he walked into a little bookshop in London and handed the manuscript of a book of poems, 'Personae,' to the owner, Elkin Mathews, who had 'discovered' Yeats.

The Evening Bulletin, Philadelphia, February 20th 1928.

to publish in his October issue a selection of poems from Williams's forthcoming book *The Tempers*. Pound contributed an introductory note which throws some light on the American poetry he had been reading: "I have greatly enjoyed *The Songs from Vagabondia* by Mr Bliss Carman and the late Richard Hovey, certain poems by Mr Cheney and a Chorus by Mr Robert Gilbert Welsh . . ."

The works of Carman and Hovey were well known in American literary circles during Pound's early years and John Vance Cheney was a figure of some note during the early part of the century. Judging by a few similarities in Pound's poetry, then and later, it seems likely that one of the books he read was Cheney's *The Time of Roses,* published in September 1908 by Thomas B. Mosher of Portland, Maine. Robert Welsh was a little known poet whom Pound had met during his stay in New York in 1910.

On March 26th 1914 the *Philadelphia Evening Bulletin* announced that "Ezra Pound, Wyncote Boy, Who Achieved Fame Abroad, Soon to Wed." The story continued: "Cable announcement of the coming marriage of Ezra Pound, the brilliant young Philadelphia poet, and Miss Dorothy Shakespear, daughter of Mr and Mrs Hope Shakespear, of London . . . has attracted attention to the brilliant career of this youth, whose early days were spent at Wyncote, in the Old York Road section."

Not all Philadelphians, however, were always enthusiastic. A correspondent called "The Gownsman," after pointing out that Philadelphia was a city full of poets ("they bustle in our streets"), concluded a later story with these remarks:

> The Gownsman will not gratify the vanity of a certain Philadelphia poet, who took his talents and his crochets away with him to London, by miscalling all these [i.e. the Philadelphia poets already mentioned in the article] "the shillings and pence of Philadelphia poets." None shall pound so ungraceful an illusion out of your Gownsman, who apologises for the scores he has left unsung.

This may have been the work of Christopher Morley (born Haverford, Pa., 1890), who at the time was one of the most successful journalists in Philadelphia. Morley moved to New York and in his column "The Bowling Green," in the *New York Evening Post* of July 2nd 1920, published the following parody of the poems in Pound's book *Cathay* (London 1915):

> When the frogs clear their throats
> Like old club members,
> And the fireflies
> Punctuate the dusk with a network of bright-
> ness,
> Hasten, boy, to his Excellency Mu-Kow,
> Ask him to join me
> In a trifling merriment.
> And be careful
> To stretch two white ropes
> Along the path,
> Lest, when His Excellency totters homeward
> in the darkness,
> He fall in the canal.
>
> (from the Chinese of No Sho)

Homer and Isabel Pound visited London in July 1914 to see their son and his bride. The First World War broke out during their stay. Dorothy Pound, in a letter of July 13th 1972, pointed out that "problems arose about their returns to U.S.A." They sailed separately and arrived back in Philadelphia before the end of 1914.

Isabel Pound was a member of the Women's Club of Wyncote and sometimes read her son's latest poems to the assembled ladies, among them Mrs Cyrus H. K. Curtis, Mrs George H. Lorimer, Mrs J. B. Stetson Jnr., and Mrs Van Court. On November 27th 1918 Mrs Van Court presented an "original poem":

> Mrs Pound was early with us
> Mother of the famous Ezra;
> Living far away in London
> Writes his verses weird and witty . . .

On December 11th that year Isabel, using material supplied by her son, gave a talk to the club on "Art and Artists in England during the War." According to the minutes of the club for December 3rd 1918 Mrs Pound's report of the meeting of the Drama League was most interesting.

Pound sometimes regretted not having his doctorate and in later years made several attempts to get one from the University of Pennsylvania. Here is Emily Mitchell Wallace's account, in her article "Penn's Poet Friends," of an approach to the university in 1920 by Homer Pound:

> In 1920, Homer Pound whom his son affectionately described as "the naivest man who ever possessed sound sense," went to the University to ask Dr Schelling, head of the English Department, whether a Ph.D. or an honorary degree might be given to his son. Since Pound appears to have earned the requisite hours of credit, and, out of the many books he had published by 1920, either *The Spirit of Romance* (1910) or his scholarly edition of the *Sonnets and Ballate of Guido Cavalcanti* (1912) surpass the standards of many a Ph.D. dissertation, the question was not unrseaonable.
>
> That Ezra actually suggested that his father visit Dr Schelling seems unlikely, though in 1920 he was preparing to leave London and was considering all sorts of things, even the study of medicine.
>
> • • • •

The meeting between Homer Pound and Felix Schelling no doubt was courteous and diplomatic. Afterwards, Dr Schelling, who had himself received two honorary degrees from the University (Litt.D., 1903, and LL.D., 1909) wrote to several people dutifully asking their opinion and offering his own:

> . . . I am sure the Faculty would not recommend that Mr Pound be granted the degree of Ph.D. for the simple reason that he has done

none of the work demanded of such a student. The question of an honorary degree for Mr Pound upon the basis of his eccentric and often very clever verse is quite another matter and one which I hardly feel that I am competent to raise.

The matter was dropped without further consideration,[1] and the University never honoured Pound in any way during his life.

In June 1928 Homer Pound retired from the Mint and he and his wife began to plan a long looked forward to trip to see their son in Italy. After twelve years in London and four in Paris, he had, in 1924, settled in Rapallo. The parents' pride had kept pace with their son's achievements and they followed his career in detail. In February 1928 Homer gave his latest news to a journalist, Mary Dixon Thayer, whose long report appeared in the *Evening Bulletin* of February 20th. The headline declared: "Ezra Pound's Father Tells How Son Went To London With a Shilling and Found Fame." The story opened with the following paragraphs:

> Not since the days of "Dick" Whittington, perhaps, has a youth with only a shilling in his pocket gone up to London Town and won fame as quickly and unexpectedly as did a young Philadelphian, Ezra Pound.
>
> "I like to talk about Ezra," said Mr Pound, smiling, as we sat in his large private office at the Mint. "I got a letter from him this morning and there's a photo of my little grandson too. He's just fourteen months old and his name is Omar after the famous poet, you know. Ezra says he wants to keep up the poetic tradition in the family."

There was always a ready welcome at the Pound home for anyone even remotely connected with Ezra. On August 16th

---

[1] Ezra Pound made a further attempt in the 1930s. N.S.

1928 the *Times Chronicle* reported that "Mr John J. Becker has been the guest of Mr and Mrs Homer Pound this week. Mr Becker is a composer and is College Advisory Director of St Mary's of the Springs, Columbus, Ohio. He has made two musical interpretations of Ezra Pound's Chinese poems which have been published in New York." The following year (May 9th 1929) the paper announced that "Mr and Mrs Homer Pound will sail for England on June 1. They will visit their son, Ezra Pound, the famous poet. Ezra Pound lived in Wyncote for many years. Mr and Mrs Pound were among the first settlers. Ezra Pound and his wife, who is a descendant of William Shakespeare, have been spending the winter with a group of celebrated writers in southern Italy." A week later the *Times Chronicle* reported that although Homer and Isabel had their return passage to America booked for October 4th, there was already a possibility that they might remain abroad indefinitely. Then on September 19th, this report: "Mr and Mrs Homer Pound . . . are now in Rapallo, Italy, where with Mr and Mrs Ezra Pound they expect to spend the winter. Ezra Pound has just written a new book which is the definitive edition of the works of Guido Cavalcanti. Mr and Mrs Homer Pound wish to dispose of their house in Wyncote and have a permanent residence abroad." Another account appeared on March 6th 1930:

> The friends of Mr and Mrs Homer Pound will be glad to know they are having a delightful winter in Rapallo, Italy, near their son Ezra Pound, the famous poet and his wife who was Miss Dorothy Shakespear and a direct descendant of "The Bard of Avon."[1]

> Mr Pound and his son expect to take a trip to Frankfort, Germany, in April for the premiere of George A n t h e i l 's opera [*Transatlantic (The Peoples Choice)*]. Antheil is a young American

---

[1]Mrs. Pound (letter to me of 13th July 1972) pointed out that the *Times-Chronicle* was wrong in ascribing direct descent: "We are descended from an uncle of Shxprs—his father's brother."

composer from Trenton, N.J. and we understand the scene of his new opera is a Child's Restaurant. We suppose therefore it is uncommonly modern.

Mrs Pound received from Miss Esther Heacock a bunch of clippings from the *Times-Chronicle* telling her news of her old friends here. We would like to quote from Mrs Pound's letter to Miss Heacock giving them a glimpse of the happy life the Pounds are leading in Italy.

"Wyncote is very lovely, but does not equal Rapallo (Italy). We now have a blue cottage amid the gray green olive trees where the birds sing, the sea chants, waves roam and splash and the mountains remain quiet, waiting for Mohammed to come to them. Flowers are in bloom in all the gardens, Narcissus, Japonica, Jonquils, Heliotrope etc. Oranges hang on their trees, we have lots of fruit, walnuts and almonds, and life goes very pleasantly."

The furnishings at 166 Fernbrook Avenue were auctioned, except for the silver and family portraits, which Mrs Van Court sent to Rapallo. Soon afterwards, in July 1930, the house itself was auctioned.

V

Following the Great Depression and economic chaos of the 1930s, Ezra Pound became attracted to some of the policies of Mussolini in Italy. He claimed at the same time that the true democracy of the American Founding Fathers was no longer being practised in the United States. Taking a line of thought that was peculiarly his own Pound criticised the American government and commented on the origins and conduct of the Second World War, in broadcasts he made over Rome Radio after the United States had entered the conflict. He was indicted for treason, but at the end of the war when he was taken to Washington a group of doctors pronounced him unfit to stand trial. As a result he spent from 1946 until 1958 in St Elizabeths Hospital for the Criminally Insane in Washington, D.C. While there he read, wrote, received a great many visitors and kept up a world-wide correspondence. In 1953 his friend T.S. Eliot (by this time a successful dramatist as well as poet and critic) paid him one of his regular visits. For the occasion Pound, whose nickname for Eliot was "Possum," composed the following quatrain:

THE DRAMATIST

(but spoken in a friendly tone 6th June 1953)

Olympian allergy to thought in all its forms
Now shields our "Possum" from the raging storms,

Both fatter and calmer, who now fills the boards
His meaning hidden in a host of words.

E. P.

One day in the summer of 1956 Pound received an unexpected letter from a young man, Carl Gatter, who with his widowed mother, Mrs Elsie Kugel Gatter, was the occupant of 166 Fernbrook Avenue. Fired by memories of old Wyncote Pound send out a stream of letters to Gatter in which he described past incidents and asked for news of survivors. On January 5th 1957 he wrote:

> Thanks for census report. Sorry Joe [Cochran] is dead, he was younger than I am.
>
> Give my undying love to Catherine [Reed, née Cochran, Joe's sister], who used to be swung under THE apple tree, with long golden hair aetat 6 or thereabouts.

As details of the past began to come back to him he sent off letters to old friends and acquaintances living in or near Wyncote. Early in 1958 several went to his former teacher, Miss Florence Ridpath, who was still alive in Jenkintown. She was glad to hear from him and recalled in her replies incidents from the old days when she was in charge of Wyncote's temporary school. Despite her advanced age Pound very characteristically tried to interest her in his plans for the reform of American universities.

He had now been in St. Elizabeths Hospital for more than twelve years and there were moves afoot to obtain his release. Among those awaiting this happy event was his daughter, Mary de Rachewiltz, who, with her father's approval, had prepared a home for him in Italy. Early in 1958 some American newspapers reported that she was planning to visit him at St. Elizabeths. Mrs Gatter wrote to Pound that she would be glad to show his daughter the family home. On March 9th 1958 Pound replied:

> Dear Mrs Gatter,
>   Thank God we aren't society people either.

Homer Pound, at Rapallo, Italy, August 1933.
(The Free Library of Philadelphia)

Ezra Pound and his daughter Mary, Venice, 1935.

Pound preparing an English version of Confucius in the dispensary of
U.S. Army's Disciplinary Training Centre, outside Pisa, Italy, where he
was imprisoned after his arrest in 1945.

Dinner at 166 Fernbrook Avenue, June 27th 1958.
(The Free Library of Philadelphia)

Wyncote, June 27th 1958.
(The Free Library
of Philadelphia)

Wyncote, June 28th 1958, shortly before Pound left for New York and Italy. (The Free Library of Philadelphia)

At his daughter's castle, Brunnenburg, Tirolo di Merano, Italy, 1959.

Brunnenburg

Rapallo

Venice

Walter and Patricia de Rachewiltz, at
Brunnenburg, February 1970.

Mary de Rachewiltz.

Mary grew up among peasants and can lead a plough horse or get up (at least she once was able to) at 5 a.m. to dig potatoes.

He forwarded the invitation to his daughter who was mistress of Brunnenburg Castle, in the village of Tirolo, high above the city of Merano, in northern Italy. Her reply arrived in Wyncote early in April:

Dear Mrs Gatter,

Thank you so much for your kind letter and the block-print which I am very happy to receive. Father once sent on a letter which your son wrote to him — a wonderful letter which filled me with longing to see the place he so vividly cherishes. And now you tell me to come with the children to see the house where my grandparents lived (grandmother often spoke of it) and where father spent his childhood. There is nothing I'd like better, and if I do come to America this summer I shall certainly pay you a visit . . . My journey now depends on whether father will be released. I have made a home for him here and we have been waiting for 12 years now, how anxiously you can well imagine! According to the papers we seem to have reasons for new hope.

Although brought up, as her father said, among peasants, Mary de Rachewiltz was now married to an Italian nobleman. She had known both Homer and Isabel during their long stay in Italy. Homer died in Italy in 1942; Isabel, cared for by her granddaughter, lived on until 1948 when she died at Schloss Neuhaus, near Gais, in the Italian Tirol. Mary de Rachewiltz did not make her proposed visit to America during the summer of 1958, for on April 18th, in a Washington court, the indictment against her father was dismissed and on May 7th he was free to leave the hospital in the custody of his wife.

Pound was now ready to return to Italy. But before he

did he revisited Wyncote and some of the scenes of his childhood and youth. Mrs Gatter invited him to spend a few days at 166 Fernbrook Avenue; on May 5th he sent a short note:

> Dear Gatters,
>
> I doubt if we will be going to N. York by car/ IF so we wd need beds for 3, and wd be delighted to stop a night in Wyncote/
>
> date of sailing not yet known. In fact haven't yet visas.
>
> cordially (but, as you may well believe somewhat crowdedly
>
> yours
>
> *Ez P*

As the time of his visit drew nearer he sent three additional letters and postcards.

> 12 May 1958
>
> Dear Mrs Gatter,
>
> Present indications are that toward end of JUNE the three of us will be being taken to N.Y. by Mr and Mrs Horton in their car.[1]
>
> I shd be delighted to spend a night at 166/ can I rent a room for the Hortons in the vicinage?
>
> Not sure of exact date yet.
>
> Offers of other rooms near Phila, but not in Wyncote.
>
> somewhat in haste
>
> yrs
>
> *E.P.*

---

[1] David Horton was a young Washington lawyer who visited Pound regularly at St. Elizabeths and, under Pound's direction, ran a small publishing firm, the Square Dollar Press.

103

The second letter was dated May 27th:

Dear Mrs Gatter,

Much rather spend night and more day if you have room for the five of us.

Thanks,

E.P.

date determinable later.

A postcard dated the following day read:

P.S. what languages do you and Carl read?

yrs

E.P.

Even while getting ready for his visit to Wyncote he was planning, it seems, to draw up a reading-list and send reading matter for the edification of his hostess and her son. Finally, on June 19th, he had definite news on his departure from Washington:

C.G.

Unless they change sailing date or some other calamity schedule now to arrive Wyncote for lunch latish on the 27th and stay to breakfast next day, or even to lunch. BUT I still want to know what foreign languages you read for pleasure, if any.

no sense distributing illegible printed matter.

yours

E.P.

I mean I spose Dave will get there for lunch or by what would be tea time in London.

Pound himself referred to this section of his return to Italy as "Wyncote Revisited." Here is Mr Gatter's recollection of it, based upon the notes he jotted down at the time:

Pound and his entourage were scheduled to arrive at Fernbrook Avenue around 7 p.m., Friday, June 27th. The party was delayed. Mrs Gatter was quite upset because the eye of the round roast was falling to pieces in the oven. About 8.5 p.m. there was a reassuring telegram from David Horton explaining that they would be late. Finally, about 9 p.m., Ezra Pound, Dorothy his wife, Mr and Mrs Horton, and Miss Marcella Spann[1] arrived. "Dave" ("my publisher," Pound called him) had become lost in the maze of suburbia. Pound wasn't upset, however, for they had passed through Valley Forge and had also driven by "Gray Towers," the home of W. W. Harrison, known as the "Sugar King," whose fortune had provided Pound's Fellowship in Romanics and trip to Europe in 1906. Pound noted that "Gray Towers" was now occupied by Beaver College.

"Dolled the place up a bit," was his first reaction as he bounded up the front walk at 166 Fernbrook Avenue. He entered and walked quickly from room to room. Everyone followed and watched intently. He pulled the sliding-doors that led to the front parlour, and, as he ascended the stairs, grabbed an oak finial on the newel post which came away in his hand. It had, he explained, been unfastened when he was a boy.

The stained glass window on the landing was still cracked from his tennis practice in the side yard. The window must have been repaired quite early. The pieces have been carefully leaded by a skilled craftsman.

On the second floor he inspected his first bedroom, the "tower room." It was there, in the closet, that his mother had, for a few minutes, placed him as a punishment. Pound next inspected his parents' front chamber, and the large middle room which probably had once been used as a sitting-room. Accompanied by Carl Gatter he then made a groping search in the back yard for remembered trees, after which they walked to the street and untied the suitcases from the top of Horton's car.

Around 9.30 p.m. everyone sat down for dinner. A

---

[1]A young woman from Texas, co-editor with Pound of the anthology *Confucius to Cummings* (N.Y. 1964).

wicker wing-chair was carried from the back parlour, because, as Horton explained, "grandpop's head needs the support." Pound commented on the quality of the roast and on the chemical-free taste of the Springfield water. When I mentioned that it was fifty years since he had last supped at 166, he said softly, "yes, my semi-centennial." Throughout dinner he talked constantly and frequently quoted phrases that Yeats had spoken. Miss Spann and the others appeared fatigued. David Horton, however, listened closely and hung on his every word like a devoted disciple.

At the conclusion of the meal Pound removed his glasses and posed for colour photographs. He then presented the Gatters with copies of some of his works. In one he wrote "Wyncote revisited June 28, '58."

While Mrs Pound, Mrs Horton and Marcella Spann were helping with the dishes, Pound rested on the front parlour sofa and answered my questions about his early life. "The Ballad of the Goodly Fere" was written, he told me, "to answer London sceptics." With great emotion he mentioned the "gorilla cage" in which he had been imprisoned by the American Army in Italy. He also had a few questions himself. "What about the patent?" This was a cast-iron device constructed within the rear parlour fireplace. It sent heated air to the parlour and to the room directly above. Unfortunately "the patent" had set the house ablaze and was removed.

All retired except Pound and his interviewer. Later he indicated that he wished to remain on the sofa. As I entered my bedroom I heard the front door open and close. Pound walked south on Fernbrook Avenue to Calvary Presbyterian Church. He and a friend had once planted an evergreen tree behind the church, but now, late at night, he was hesitant to venture on the property to learn if it still survived. The following day he said that "except for the colours of the houses," and the tremendous growth of trees and shrubbery, the Wyncote he had known remained.

The chirping of the birds was especially strong and

beautiful Saturday morning. Pound was hunting oatmeal in the kitchen before any of the others went downstairs. At breakfast everyone ate the raspberries which Priscilla and Esther Heacock had picked from their garden for the occasion. Pound appeared transformed. He forgot about the need to rest his head and sat on a regular diningroom chair. He also neglected to remove his glasses when photographed. This change in personality was noted by everyone. David Horton was amazed and slightly perplexed.

Following breakfast Pound proceeded to examine more closely the first floor. He was obviously pleased with the interior decoration and began to relate objects to the past. The large, modern, Italian madonna in the style of Luca della Robbia prompted him to mention the "world's largest" Della Robbia at Pisa which had been completely destroyed during World War II. He fondled a cast-iron candle-holder on the hall bookcase. The Pounds had possessed a similar pair and by coincidence a dragon-wing was missing, just as on theirs. On the porch he rapidly swung a tiny ladder-back rocker to eye-level. Except for the larger knobs, it might have been his own.

The poet then showed his wife the garden. He looked in a crawl-space beneath the former pantry and pulled out an old hockey stick which he thought had been his. He kissed his wife under the apple-tree. His sandals were wet with dew. He removed them and walked barefoot in the yard. When Mrs Pound retired to the porch and I drove off for provisions he remained with his memories in the yard.

When I returned he was occupying a white wicker settee with Miss Spann. Mr. Tobie, a neighbour, crossed the hedge with his dog "Cocoa." "Cocoa" licked his Mr Pound's feet, but the poet did not object. Sitting there in the yard he eloquently described old Wyncote. While learning to drive he had broken the steering on a horseless carriage. Next door was the Sheip boy forever repeating "My father makes cigar boxes." He recalled sadly that Sheip had taken all the honours when they attended Cheltenham Military Academy.

Pound returned to the house and searched the telephone directory for the names of old friends and acquaintances. The night before we had told him that his visit had been kept a secret because of our fear of having too many newspapermen at the house. I said jokingly then even the *Times-Chronicle* would have sent somebody. It was then that Pound spoke of the *Times-Chronicle* as "my first publisher." This fact he also mentioned in a letter written from Rapallo on June 11th 1959.

On Friday evening it had seemed that he wanted privacy. By Saturday afternoon he was annoyed that no one had come to visit him. Once again I explained that with the exception of the Heacocks who had accidently learned of his visit, his presence in Wyncote was unknown. Pound had little success in telephoning. Many of the town's residents were vacationing or out for the day. He chatted at length with Adele Polk. Another old friend, Mrs Reed, was away but he was pleased to talk with her daughter. About 1.30 p.m. there was a light lunch. Pound especially liked the freshly baked rye bread. Priscilla and Esther Heacock arrived during the meal. They pretended to have "just dropped by," but the visit had been prearranged. Priscilla asked, "May I call you *Ra?*" "Well, I've been called worse things," Pound replied.

After lunch we set out for the Pound's next destination, Hopewell, New Jersey. I drove, with Pound and Miss Spann in the front, Mrs Pound and Mrs Gatter in the rear. The Hortons followed behind in their own car. The poet was silent as we descended Fernbrook Avenue. At the bottom of the hill he pointed out the "temporary" public school. The very commercialized main street of Jenkintown had changed greatly since his boyhood. On York Road he looked in vain for Miss Elliott's Dame's School. Grace Presbyterian Church had been completely rebuilt. At Willow Grove we turned eastward on to Route 158. Beyond Hatboro sprawled handsome Bucks County farms. Pound was especially interested in the early architecture of the area. At Hopewell David Horton telephoned to their next host, Alan C. Collins, who arrived shortly in a Cadillac to pick them up. Mr Collins mentioned that Homer Pound had been his Sunday school teacher. The Pounds thanked us for our hospitality and then left with Mr Collins.

Thus ends Carl Gatter's account of "Wyncote Revisited." The Pounds, accompanied by Miss Spann, left New York by ship on June 30th and arrived at Brunnenburg on July 12th. There Pound met his grandchildren Walter and Patrizia for the first time. Among the paintings at Brunneberg were the portraits of Mary Parker and greatgrandmother How, from Wyncote. And there was sometimes a touch of America in the evening menus drawn up and decorated by Patrizia:

Brunnenburg 21 Dicembre [1958]
Menu della Sera
minestra d'orzo
formaggio
apple-pie

Both Pound and his wife continued to correspond occasionally with the Gatters during the next year or so. On March 15th 1960 Mrs Pound wrote from Brunnenburg:

Ezra in Rome with a friend [Ugo Dadone] since January. The cold here too much for him. I fled to Rapallo in January and hope to get back there next week. Ezra hasn't been too well — very up and down — depressed by world outlook, and I don't wonder . . . I am so glad to have seen Ezra's old home — and he certainly was. Saluti cordiali.

Pound later became ill. After his recovery he settled into a fairly steady routine, living part of the time in Venice and the rest in Rapallo, with visits to Paris, Greece and London. He was looked after now by Miss Olga Rudge, the mother of his daughter. Miss Rudge, a concert violinist in her younger days, had been born in Youngstown, Ohio, but had spent most of her life in France and Italy. In June 1969 Pound and Miss Rudge paid a short visit to the United States, during which they were driven from New York to Philadel-

Ezra Pound and Olga Rudge visiting the Heacock sisters at Stapeley Hall, a Quaker home for the aged, 6300 Greene St., Germantown, on the outskirts of Philadelphia in June 1969. Left to right: Esther Heacock, Pound, Olga Rudge, Priscilla Heacock. Photograph taken by Pound's grandson, Walter de Rachewiltz.

phia by their grandson Walter Siegfried de Rachewiltz, who was studying at Rutgers University. At Stapeley Hall, a Quaker home for old people on the outskirts of Philadelphia, they visited the Heacock sisters, Priscilla, aged 85, and Esther, 88. The Heacocks not only knew Pound but through a cousin, the naturalist Ernest Harold Baynes, they were related by marriage to Miss Rudge. Also present during the visit was Mrs J. Stewart Smith, daughter of Joseph Linden Heacock. Mrs. Smith said that Pound was "a quiet old man" who said only a few words, leaving it to Miss Rudge to carry the conversation. Pound presented the Heacocks with a copy of his *Selected Poems* inscribed in his own hand:

for Esther
and Priscilla
affectionately
Ezra
June 15 — 1969
Wyncote

After Walter had taken some photographs of the group Mrs Smith explained to him how to drive through Wyncote on the way back to New York. It was Pound's last visit to Pennsylvania. He and Miss Rudge returned to Europe on June 18th and continued to live quietly in Venice, where, on November 1st 1972, he died at the age of 87. He was buried on the nearby cemetery island of San Michele.

P3

EZRA POUND'S PENNSYLVANIA
WAS DESIGNED BY THOMAS DURNFORD
JOANNE JOYS AND SANDRA KEIL OF THE
UNIVERSITY OF TOLEDO PUBLICATIONS OFFICE
IT WAS SET IN 12 POINT CASLON BY TOLEDOTYPE INC.
PRINTED IN DECEMBER 1975 ON 70 POUND WARREN'S OLD STYLE
BY PRINTERS THREE INC. OF TOLEDO OHIO
AND PUBLISHED BY THE FRIENDS OF THE
UNIVERSITY OF TOLEDO LIBRARIES
IN JANUARY 1976 IN AN
EDITION OF 1000
NUMBERED
COPIES

THIS IS COPY NUMBER
184